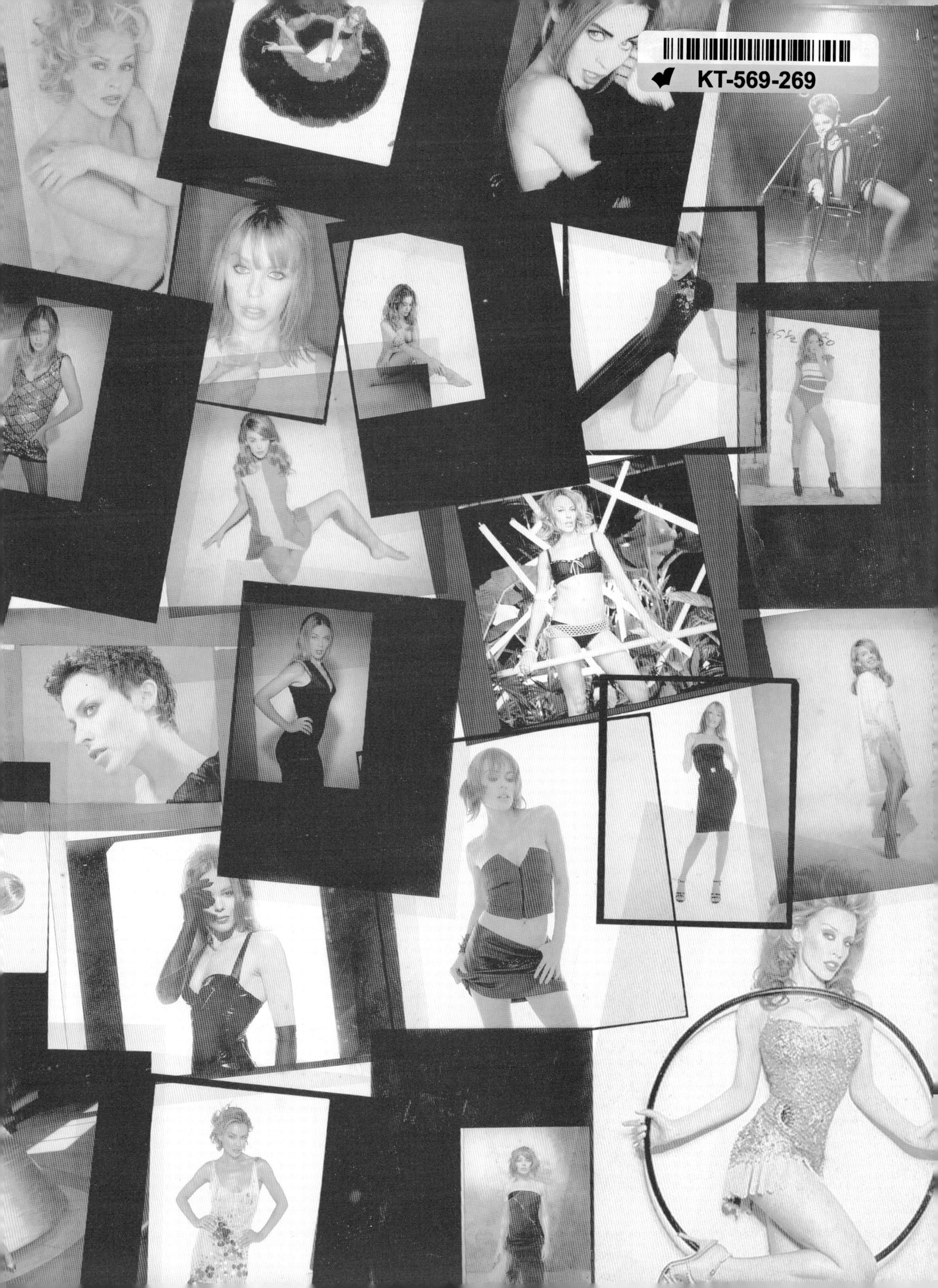

Kylie

:

La la la
William
Baker
&
Kylie
Minogue

Hodder & Stoughton

First published in Great Britain
in 2002 by Hodder and Stoughton
A division of Hodder Headline

A CIP catalogue record for this
title is available from the
British Library

ISBN 0 340 73439 6

Colour reproduction by Radstock
Reproductions Ltd, Midsomer Norton.

Printed and bound in Great
Britain by Butler & Tanner Ltd,
Frome, Somerset.

Hodder and Stoughton
A division of Hodder Headline
338 Euston Road
London NW1 3BH

Preface
&
Introduction

005-015

Diamonds are a girl's best friend.

Photography by Jul...

(handwritten) our hearts ache for friendship.

MINOGUE, KYLIE

Delicate, timeless, involved, boundless. Friends give meaning to emotion... eed experience... become a physical part o... me, they teach... about the world and myself. I have laughed and cried with Willie, we are partners in crime, he understands me when I don't and he's my favourite handbag. Our hearts ache for friendship

BAKER, WILLIAM

My friendship with Kylie is unconditional. The ... ting of t...so... tone. ...e brightens up my life more than any diama... e I glue onto her tiara and she gives me confid... ce, love and respect. I feel honoured and grateful when she dances through my life... I have been, and ever shall be, her friend

Playing what is known as "the stupidest game on earth".

'Celebrity is about fantasy.'
Alison Jackson

I met Kylie in 1994 when I was
working at Vivienne Westwood's
flagship boutique on Conduit
Street, London. I leapt from
behind the counter and bombarded
her with ideas and she agreed to
accompany me to a coffee shop
across the road. 'He did all the
talking and nothing's changed,'
she remarked recently about that
initial meeting. I was surprised
at her trust in a stranger and
she seemed flattered by my
interest, scribbling her phone
number on a napkin and signing it
'Miss K'.
   There began a friendship that
has already lasted for nine
years. Kylie is a best friend,
confidante and muse. For the best
part of a decade we have grown up
together, worked together,
laughed together and cried
together. Her presence in my life
has shaped my journey to an
extent that I cannot put into
words. Without her, life would be
a dull place.
   I began working with her as a
stylist shortly after we met.
Kylie and her then flatmate,
Katerina Jebb, would often stage
impromptu photo shoots in the
Chelsea apartment or wherever
they were at the time. I wasn't
allowed to attend the first
shoot, but they took the clothes
that I had gathered from my
boyfriend's attic, leftovers from
his days as a punk, and from the
Westwood press office.

   Shortly after, Kat, Kylie and
I became close friends. Kat had
encouraged me to style many of
her photo shoots and the three of
us struck an almost instant
rapport. Kat's unique aesthetic
and barking personality made her
the ideal teacher for me and I
learned so much from her. Murray
Blewett and Mark Spye, who worked
in the Westwood studio and with
whom I lived at the time, had
given me a condensed cultural and
fashion history of the latter
half of the twentieth century.
They taught me about the eighties
club scene, about legendary
nightclubs, The Blitz and Taboo,
about the uniqueness of London
style and panache, about
Vivienne's early history, about
punk, about Warhol and about the
chic and cheap deco brilliance of
Barbara Hulanicki's Biba label,
of which Murray was a fanatic
collector. They taught me how to
look at clothes, how to wear
them, and how they could look on
others. They had been responsible
for many of the Boy London
designs that I had worn so
fervently as a teenage Boy George
fan, and I felt like I was in the
presence of my heroes. I learned
so much more than I would ever
have done at college had I
studied fashion design or a
related subject. I learned as I
went along.
   Through milliner Philip
Treacy, who had been a friend for
some time, I met stylist Isabella
Blow. I assisted Issy for a few
months, which opened my eyes even
more to fashion. I developed a
love and respect for the very
English eccentric, and her unique
perspective and sublime aesthetic
informed and taught me about the
glamour of couture, about
decadent excess, and about a more
surreal yet refined approach to
style. I found styling
individuals came easily and quite
naturally to me. I could draw on
my own experience, my own
aesthetic and my own developing
tastes.

When it came to working within the context of a fashion magazine, however, I found things more difficult. My inspiration flows naturally from people that I know, from a subject I am familiar with. It was fine if I knew something about the subject, if the model was a friend or someone I had a perception of, but I found it difficult to grasp what fashion editor Katie Grand referred to as a more 'conceptual' aproach to fashion. I was never happy with the shoots I did for *Dazed & Confused, The Face* and *i-D*, and neither was anyone else.

Having spent time with Issy, Philip and Katie, and other people who worked in the industry, I realised through trial and error that I wasn't really cut out to be a 'fashion' stylist – my ideas often had no relevance to the fashionable climate of the time. I interpreted clothes literally rather than conceptually, and naively saw them as a means of dressing something up and not as important in themselves. Time changed this perception, but back then the fashion industry wore my already fragile ego down. I found it frustrating that someone else could hold power over what I thought was good or bad, what was 'cool' and what was 'uncool'. I found the fashion world was a cut-throat place, and I never felt truly secure there, adoring the glamorous world of the Paris catwalks but despising the snobbery and competition of the industry, despite being both snobbish and competitive myself.

My real interest lay not in fashion but in pop. Pop art, pop music, anything pop. Even my dog is called Poppy. In my work, pop was my salvation. Pop and pop stars enabled me to have more freedom and subsequent satisfaction in my own brand of self-expression. I worked with Garbage, Tricky, PJ Harvey and Jamiroquai, amongst others. I found it satisfying to give something back to artists whose work I respected, to play a part in and contribute to a pop culture that has shaped and continues to shape my life.

Nothing came much poppier than Kylie. When I first met her I was in the middle of the first year of a degree course in Theology. I am not remotely religious and had absolutely no intention of becoming a priest. My university career was driven by the simple objective of getting to London and I studied at King's College, waltzing out three years later with a respectable 2:2, not bad for someone who had spent the last three years and all his student loans devouring the fashions that London offered. It was on one such shopping spree that I accidentally landed at Westwood, where I struck up a conversation with the then manager, Derek Dunbar, who had incidentally doubled for David Bowie in a shower scene in the film *The Hunger*.

My dabbling in religious theory is not really at odds with my current occupation as Kylie's creative director. To me, there was a latent mystery and power in the language and imagery of religion. As a pop fan and a child of the MTV generation, the connections between pop and celebrity and religion seemed obvious. Like religion, pop was an opiate of the masses. Reproductions of pop icons and celebrity idols had replaced religious imagery as the dominant form of iconography in the late twentieth century. Tribes of loyal fans follow a pop idol, a footballer or a movie star with the same devotion that once characterised religious faith. Pop music, like religion, expresses codes and doctrines through the emotions of a lyric or through the voice of the singer. Each fan interprets their own feelings through the sentiments expressed in their favourite song by their favourite artist.

Belief in a hero or heroine endows the star with superhuman qualities, their idealised image commanding worship, often with the celebrity's persona becoming a mask behind which they attempt to live normal lives. Kylie does not go shopping in gold hot pants. The image of a celebrity is a deliberate construction. Religion works in the same way, through subliminal suggestion and seduction, a testament to the 'charismatic authority' of the divine presence in question. Even the terms 'idol' and 'icon', so often applied to a celebrity, are religiously loaded. Icon is a word that Kylie feels uncomfortable with, describing herself as a 'watery icon' after the dilution of the true meaning of the word by today's *Hello!* magazine's voyeuristic and titillating culture.

Pop icons and the images they produce have always captivated me. I grew up with Madonna and Boy George, two champions of the philosophy of self-reinvention, their own chameleon instincts inherited from the pop generation which had worshipped at the platform shoes of David Bowie. Their image changes are not just superficial, they are deep-set revolutions of identity, achieved through the manipulation of clothing and make-up. Kylie is such an artist, a manipulator of image and audience.

This book is a celebration of modern iconography and the evolution of a contemporary pop star. From her roots in a Melbourne soap opera to her most recent tour, KylieFever2002, it is an unashamed homage to pop's schizophrenia and the multiple identities contained within the tiny body of Kylie Minogue.

The images in this book are presented here because they are worthy of being presented. They are hopefully a testament of their times and an indelible record of a life spent for the most part in front of the camera lens, be it on a photo session, the set of a video, in a television studio or through the prying lens of a paparazzi.

This book is also a thank you to the many people who work behind the scenes: the designers who make the clothes; the make-up artists and hairdressers; the photographers; the video directors; lighting men; graphic designers; stylists; record companies; management and the fans; all who have turned Kylie Ann Minogue into the international brand that she has become. These images have been produced not just by an individual, but by a team of unsung talent that has moulded and shaped Kylie's visual identity over the years. This book belongs to all these collaborators.

Pop is not brain surgery or rocket science but it plays an important role in the twenty-first century in providing entertainment, distraction and escapism. I hope you find at least one of those things here.

William Baker
September 2002

SOUTH
OAKLEIGH
KINDERGARTEN
1972

CAMBERWELL
HIGH SCHOOL
YEAR 7B
1980

THE He

Photos are a direct line from me to you. I've been fortunate enough to work with some of the most talented and respected photographers whose artistry I am so thankful for. I've been involved in good, bad and ugly pictures and they all have their place. Some will stand the test of time. Others just satisfy a superficial and passing empty space in a newspaper or magazine but they are all powerful. Some say more than words ever could, some show the cold, hard facts and there are some which pave the way for absurd commentary to turn the viewer's perspective of a genuine image into something far from its concept. In my experience the camera is both friend and foe, but whether I love or loathe it, it is and has been an inescapable and a major part of my life.

At worst I never want to see another one again and at best I want to work with it, to push its boundaries, to collaborate with like-minded people on the artistic and social impact of an image.

This book was originally intended to be one of photographs and various pictorial images, mostly relating to style. I decided that the pictures would benefit from some text to give them another aspect, shed some light on how they came to be or to offer a purely historical aside.

As we delved into seemingly endless boxes with folders of negs and contact sheets, prints, Polaroids, tear sheets, stats and costume sketches and all manner of memorabilia, it became perfectly clear that every picture did indeed have a story to tell. Some are better left untold so sometimes here you may only have the finished image to spark an emotion or the imagination. Others led to further stories and before I knew it there were tangled tentacles of humour, intrigue, the disastrous and experimental, iconic, ironic, simple, ridiculous, spur of the moment, brilliant and banal, of people, places, history, highs and lows, and I wondered how on earth this could still be the simple picture book we set out to make. It couldn't.

I was adamant I didn't want this to become a life story, though it has become biographical in content. I'm not ready for the whole shebang. I have long successfully avoided the almost inevitable autobiography. This is because I feel so much of it deserves to be left private. I also didn't feel there was much of a story to tell. I mean, where would I start and finish when in many ways I feel I am just beginning? I'm interested in the future, not the past.

However, in the process of putting this book together, memories have unfolded from the images we unearthed. Far too many to be ignored. (And far too many to be confined by the pages of this book) They are worth sharing if only in respect of the people I have met and the experiences we have shared. Ordinary stories can be extraordinary. It's the human condition to be fascinated by other people. One of these people is the unique William Baker. He is a natural storyteller and will no doubt lure you into his way of viewing the world. In this case 'Kylieworld'. He is a most qualified commentator as a best friend, creative collaborator and pop culture junkie.

As I mentioned my life story will have to wait, but in the meantime here are some anecdotes, explanations, perhaps revelations and, of course, photos.

Please enjoy and know that it is your enjoyment that has played a major part in allowing me to come this far.

Love to you all,

Kylie x

01

:

The
disco
diva
next
door

Thats where it started.
I was in people's living
rooms or kitchens twice
a day, for two and a
half years acting out
day-to-day dramas in
a soap opera. I think
people thought of me as
a distant relative as a
result of 'Neighbours'

I was always a fan of soap opera. Like most teenage homos with delusions of grandeur and dreams of a huge mansion and a warring extended family, I was gripped by the American supersoaps of the eighties. Joan Collins' one-liners and waspish repartee ranging from 'I'll destroy you for what you did to me, Blake Carrington' and 'Damn you, Blake', through to her shrieking 'Get off me Krystle, you crazy cow!' as her wig was being pulled askew, became essential learning for me. Much of my life was interpreted through the language of soap. Faced with any teenage drama or crisis, I would glare in the mirror in some angst-ridden pose and imagine bold yellow type over my face in the style of *Dynasty*'s freeze-frame cliffhangers. Women were celebrated as powerful creatures of glamour and instinct, scheming, surviving and often winning in a world dominated by sex-hungry men with penchants for blue rinses.

Life for me became divided into episodes as some of the storylines of my youth were resolved and others weren't. The supersoaps were pure, ritzy, melodramatic escapism that captured to perfection the spirit of early eighties excess and materialism, with little bearing on English reality. Women adored them due to their post-feminist portrayals of the fairer sex in a Britain that was pretty much ruled by its own Iron Lady, even though no amount of pancake base, furs and shoulder pads could conceal the fact that most of these TV characters were divorced, single or alcoholics and all the families totally dysfunctional. But that was the point.

However, these glorious homages to American glamour grew tired as plots became more and more absurd as the eighties progressed. Even I found it hard to relate to a whole family being mowed down by Moldavian terrorists, and much as I would have liked it and hard as I may have wished, no UFO ever came down to rescue me from provincial teenage life. Television responded to glamour's swansongs with a new wave of soap: the ultra real.

EastEnders was devised as a prime-time slice of such realism and swiftly became a national obsession, but its harsh and often depressing storylines failed to provide the fabulous escape that so many viewers, especially teenagers, longed for. The answer came in the form of an import from the other side of the world, not America this time, but from a land that many of the British had all but forgotten: Down Under.

Neighbours quickly formed part of my daily routine and that of most of my contemporaries. It started as a twice-daily soap that formed part of the BBC's new daytime schedule, which replaced traditional educational programming and was pitched at bored housewives and pensioners. The BBC switchboard and post room were inundated with demands to shift *Neighbours*' airtime due to the number of kids who were apparently bunking off school for their daily slice of Ramsey Street life. Fifteen years later, after the Ozzie TV invasion that followed *Neighbours*, it is hard to imagine the box without that optimistic presence of Australian sunshine to brighten our dreary, rainy days with tales of intrigue and shenanigans of blonde surfies and tanned ripe-breasted, white-socked schoolgirls whose hemlines rose ever upwards with each year of transmission. Back in the early eighties, all we had to go on for a picture of Australian life was the dyke-tastic *Prisoner Cell Block H* and *Sons and Daughters*, remarkable not only for their theme tunes, but also for the bleakness of the sets, which always seemed to be in varying shades of grey, and the ugliness of the actors.

Neighbours was a ray of light
that captivated a generation with
an equally irritating theme tune
but also a cast remarkable for
their likeable normality.
Neighbours was the closest thing
at the time to interactive TV,
pre-*Big Brother*, pre-*Survivor*,
pre-*Temptation Island*. These
characters were in our homes
twice a day, looking out at us
from the one-eyed guru in the
corner of our living rooms. We
participated in the lives of the
Ramsey Street residents. In
return, as is the nature of TV,
the characters entered the lives
of the viewers. The characters,
like the actors, quickly became
public property and subsequently
tabloid fodder. Britain was
hooked.

Australian philosophy was
immortalised by *Neighbours*. Just
as the Brits coped with their
daily woes by putting the kettle
on, our Ozzie *Neighbours'*
attitude to problems was equally
simplistic and usually tackled
with one of three solutions: open
a tinny, have a barbie or jump in
the pool. Often it was all three.
Early *Neighbours* storylines have
become deeply ingrained on my
generation: tales of Daphne the
stripper's fight to be accepted
as proprietor of the coffee shop,
the mecca of all Ramsey Street's
gossip; Melbourne's acid-tongued
but less glamorous version of a
superbitch, the fabulous Mrs
Mangle, immortalised for ever by
wannabe artist Helen Daniel's
meerkat-like portrait; Bouncer
the Labrador and the comings and
goings at the Waterhole,
Melbourne's answer to the Rover's
Return, as well as the dirty
dealings of Ramsey Street's own
J.R. Ewing, Paul Robinson.

Even now it would be difficult
to find somebody who couldn't hum
the theme tune. *Neighbours* was a
simplistic picture of suburban
Melbourne life set in a street
that could have been Brookside
Close rather than on the other
side of the world. If anything,
it was this similarity, apart
from the weather, to the post-
Thatcher Wimpey and Barratt home
way of life that made it work
here. But it was the kids amongst
the cast who made *Neighbours* such
a phenomenon.

Scott Robinson, with his ever-
growing mullet hairdo and
fetching range of Speedos, played
by Jason Donovan; lost ragamuffin
schoolboy Mike, played by Guy
Pearce; plain Jane superbrain,
the swot who turned into Miss
Melbourne once she removed her
glasses; and above all, it was
Charlene Mitchell, the savvy
tomboy mechanic, who truly
captured our hearts.

Neighbours

'Neighbours' and it's environment was an incredible learning curve. It quickly reinforced the etiquette I had started to learn years before as a nine-year-old in 'Skyways' and 'The Sullivans' and a sixteen-year-old in 'The Henderson Kids'. It also paved the way for easy assimilation into the PWL Hit Factory. In soap it isn't about you; it's about teamwork and making the most of a situation. The sets wobble and sometimes your character's story-line doesn't make sense and you wish you could have more than a couple of takes, but the red light goes on and you do your best. Over the years I've had to amend some of those ingrained lessons and now, for the most part those days are over. I don't have to settle for 'OK', I'm usually in a position to make things as good as possible.

Scott and Charlene quickly became the nation's darlings as their rocky romance blossomed despite Charlene nicking a baby, having her caravan burned down and, of course, opposition from both sets of parents. Not that any of that bothered her. Charlene was a new breed of female character: feisty, independent and naturally cute. She was never plastered in war paint and didn't seem to even own a hairbrush. Nor was she ever a 'bitch'. She was literally the girl-next-door. Boys fancied her and girls either wanted to be her or be her friend.

Together, Charlene and Scott became love's young dream, a simple but lasting symbol of love conquering all, and they became the patron saints of all dating teenage couples. It was the end of an era when they packed their bags and moved to Brisbane. As far as *Neighbours* was concerned they might as well have moved to darkest Peru... they never graced Ramsey Street's wobbling sets again. But Britain did not mourn, for the Brits had claimed them as their own. Scott and Charlene Robinson had become everybody's best friends.

Brian Walsh, who at the time was at the helm of Australia's Network Ten's publicity department, also cites the Ramsey Street kids as the reason for the series' success. *Neighbours* had been axed by Channel 7, then bought by Channel 10, where it lived at first under constant threat of cancellation:

'I was given four weeks to turn things around and capture a sizeable portion of the television audience, and ensure that *Neighbours* and the network was on top. There is absolutely no doubt that if it hadn't been for Kylie, Guy Pierce, Jason, Peter O'Brien (Shane Ramsey), Elaine Smith (Daphne) et al., it simply wouldn't have worked. It would have become another casualty of the fickle nature of the Australian TV industry. They had a spirit. An Australian spirit of grit, determination, passion, hard work and fun.'

Soap opera as a genre of television has a long history of creating strong female icons, a direct response to the largely female audience who tune in regularly to escape from their household chores: *Dynasty*'s Alexis Carrington Colby Dexter, her name a reflection of the evolving divorce laws which released such women from long or often short terms of marital bondage; *Coronation Street*'s Bet Lynch, who glamorised the tarty working-class blonde; and *Prisoner Cell Block H*'s Bea Smith and the Freak who could cause even those males with the strongest of constitutions to run for cover.

Neighbours' Charlene Mitchell was a child of her times. Fiercely independent, suitably feisty, she was a feminine girl who did boys' things. Her on-screen wardrobe of oil-stained khaki dungarees made an indelible impression on both male and female viewers. Fifteen years later, Kylie's record company was elated when the tomboy image of Charlene was resurrected, minus the grease stains and with a banana-yellow pair of Dolce & Gabbana stilettos, for the video for 'Love At First Sight', as if the tomboy Charlene image symbolised the 'real' Kylie: character and actress blurred into one.

For those who grew up with *Neighbours*, Charlene is still perceived to be an intrinsic part of the package that is Kylie today. There were and are definite similarities between the two. Like Charlene, Kylie is always ready to muck in, be it sewing sequins and tassels on the hot pants and other costumes or working as a team player in her hands-on involvement with crews, on video shoots or behind the scenes on her own shows. Like Charlene, Kylie has a penchant for slapping people around the face and I have been on the receiving end of this more than once. Although not as aggressive as Charlene, Kylie, when pushed, can also see red. In a Sydney bar after a show on her Intimate and Live tour whilst playing a game of pool, a gaggle of wisecracking drag queens were the recipients of a pool cue brandished in their faces after they made one joke too many about her playing skills.

Kylie and Charlene quickly became pin-ups, her Lolita-like innocence and tumbling blonde curls combined with faux macho oil smears on her cheeks made her into an unlikely sex symbol. She was a Cinderella of the garage.

I loved playing Charlene. She was feisty and rebellious and, as is the nature of soap opera, full of surprises. With her determination to be a car mechanic she became something of a high school feminist figure. Fresh out of school and fairly determined myself, she was easy to relate to.

Kylie Minogue took the heavy workload in her stride. Since accepting the role of Charlene in February 1986 straight after leaving school, she became accustomed to success, even if it had initially surprised her. The gruelling shooting schedule of a soap that demanded five episodes a week meant that Kylie had little time to develop her own personality or do much else except play Charlene. She handled her role with ease and with what would become the consummate professionalism that anyone who works with her testifies to.

There was no time to screw up a scene, so her skills in front of the camera were honed quickly – one take is all it takes. By March of the following year she received the first of many awards: a silver Logie for Most Popular Actress in Australia. Hysteria ensued and later that year she was mobbed by hordes of fans at a personal appearance at a Sydney shopping centre. The English and Australian press were gripped by *Neighbours* mania and speculation was rife as to whether Scott and Charlene's screen romance was mirrored by 'real' life.

With distance from those days I can now appreciate them much more. As a cast, particularly the younger ones, we worked hard not only on the show, but doing all sorts of publicity. We were kept happy by the small thrill of having our hotel and mini-bar bills taken care of. We appeared at shopping malls, blue-light discos, breakfast TV, lunchtime TV and all other TVs, hospital visits, community fun days, pet sanctuaries and smiled repeatedly for endless photo shoots. I don't think any of us could understand the serious amounts of money we were helping people raise or make. We were young and up for anything.

Such charity and promotional events and personal appearances in shopping malls were par for the course for the *Neighbours* cast. The fact that Kylie appeared alongside co-stars Jason Donovan et al. cemented public opinion that their characters were real people.

Some of the Neighbours cast were always eager to help out and indulge their musical interests, so we agreed to perform at a football fundraiser. There were about eight of us. We had rehearsed a song at someone's home after work to perform on the night. We had such fun on the stage that we all wanted to do out and do another song. That song was 'The Locomotion'. After the show, in one of the quirky moments of fate that have shaped my life and career, Greg Petherick, who produced a night-time music programme at Channel 10, congratulated me on the show and suggested I make a record. I was immediately dazzled by the prospect of not only recording, but making a video. Soon after I was signed to Mushroom Records.

Kylie Minogue, pop star, was born. As well as earning her the rather unflattering nickname of the 'Singing Budgie', a moniker that proved difficult to dust off, 'The Locomotion' was recorded and became the highest selling Australian single of the decade, giving Mushroom Records their first Number One in both New Zealand and Australia. Ron Minogue, Kylie's father, had a keen business acumen and was well aware of the potential slings and arrows of outrageous pop fortune and wanted to find someone trustworthy to manage his daughter's expanding career. The answer to Ron's worries came in the shape of Terry Blamey, who still manages Kylie to this day:

'Living in Melbourne in the eighties, I was of course aware of the phenomenon that was *Neighbours*. It was also very clear to me that Kylie was the star of the show, even from the beginning in 1986. Kylie exhibited a camera presence that few in the world are fortunate to possess. She has an amazing presence, a movie star quality and has always had an incredible ability to project her personality into the minds, hearts and souls of her audiences – you cannot help but like this girl! So when her father called me one day to introduce himself and asked if I would like to discuss the possibility of representing her, I didn't hesitate for a second. I had then, and have had ever since and will continue to have, a strong belief in her ability as a truly exceptional entertainer; she has since proven herself to be a woman of extraordinary talent and ability, who knows how, and when, to use it. So, yes... I was interested in managing her.'

Kylie's musical and performing skills had begun early in her childhood. Her mum, Carol, a trained ballet dancer, encouraged all her children in the art of expression. At an under-eights' early piano competition, Kylie, after plonking her diminutive form down on a piano stool, feet barely reaching the pedals, turned to face her examiners. Placing her hands on the keyboard, fingers unable to spread to an octave, back perfectly arched, every inch a showgirl, she flirtatiously bestowed one of her trademark toothy grins on the examiners. The first prize went to a Chinese whizzkid, and Kylie trundled home with a second place certificate and, to this day, her father thinks it was the smile that sealed the deal. She instinctively knew how to work an audience, even when most little girls were in sand pits or knotting their Girls World's hair. The little lady always was a tramp.

Kylie is annoyingly good at everything she turns her hand to. If I had been at school with her, I'm sure I would have kicked her down the corridor many times as she received gold star after gold star. Her quick adaptability and versatility were evident in her youthful musical experiments.

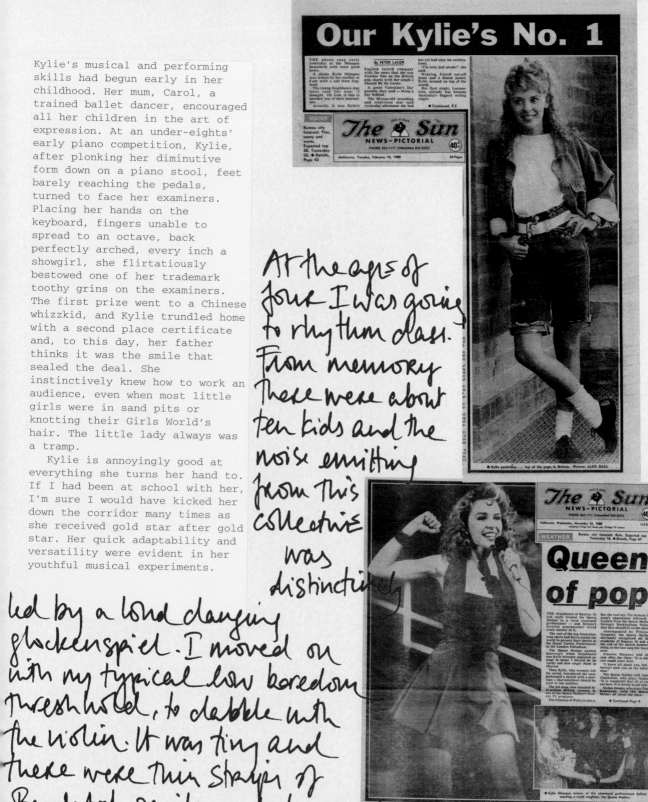

Our Kylie's No. 1

By PETER LALOR

THE phone rang early yesterday at the Minogue household with some good news.

A sleepy Kylie Minogue was woken by her mother at 4 am with a call from England.

The young Neighbours star later told The Sun: "I thought, 'Oh God, if this is another one of those journalists...'

"Actually, it was Kylie's

English record company with the news that she was Number One on the British pop charts with her single I Should Be So Lucky.

A great Valentine's Day present, they said — being a day behind.

The 19-year-old television star said yesterday afternoon she had

not yet had time for celebrations.

"I'm only just awake!" she said.

Wearing frayed cut-off jeans and a denim jacket, Kylie seemed on top of the world.

Her first single, Locomotion, already has become Australia's biggest selling single.

● Continued, P.2

The Sun
NEWS-PICTORIAL
PHONE 652-1111 (Classified 652-2222)
Melbourne, Tuesday, February 16, 1988
40c
64 Pages

● Kylie yesterday ... top of the pops in Britain. Picture: ALEX GALL

The Sun
NEWS-PICTORIAL
PHONE 652-1111 (Classified 652-2222)
Melbourne, Wednesday, November 23, 1988
40c
112 Pages

Queen of pop

THE Neighbours of Ramsay St last night treated the Queen Mother to a royal command performance — and Britain's favorite grandmother loved every minute of it.

The cast of the top Australian soap opera had flown across the world to present their sketch at the Royal Variety Performance at the London Palladium.

The Queen Mother nodded knowingly when Neighbours star Kylie Minogue appeared on stage to mime I Should Be So Lucky and sang a new single Made It In Heaven.

Then Kylie, who recently took the serial, introduced the cast, performed a sketch with a message — that neighbors should be good to one another.

The hit soap now watched by 16 million British viewers is one of the Queen Mother's favourite TV programs.

The Princess of Wales is also a

fan, the earl say. The Ramsay St gang's appearance followed a request from the Queen Mother through Buckingham Palace that they should be on the show.

Accompanied by Princess Margaret, the Queen Mother obviously recognised all the residents of Ramsay St and at the end of the sketch hummed along as the cast sang the theme tune.

Princess Margaret told the cast after the show: "It is nice you could come here."

"I love all about you, but I haven't seen you on the television."

The Queen Mother told Anne Charleston, who plays Madge: "It is wonderful that all of you are here. It is lovely to see you."

Stefan Dennis, who plays Paul Robinson, told the Queen Mother all about the show.

● Continued Page 4

● Kylie Minogue mimes at the command performance before meeting a royal neighbour, the Queen Mother.

At the age of four I was going to rhythm class. From memory there were about ten kids and the noise emitting from this collective was distinctively led by a loud clanging glockenspiel. I moved on with my typical low boredom threshold, to dabble with the violin. It was tiny and there were thin strips of Band-Aid on its neck to mark where to put my fingers. It was my violin teacher who also taught me the piano. She was quite new age and encouraged me to learn music in a way that I would enjoy. I learned to play instruments by ear.

Whilst the infant Kylie was snagging her nails on her violin strings, a musical genre that had been defined as 'Boystown', after one of its early ambassadors, had become the dominant sound in gay clubs all over England. Ian Levine, record producer and resident DJ at Heaven, London's biggest gay club, had re-christened the new trashy disco sound 'Hi-NRG'. It was a fusion of white and black vocals, formulaic metronomic beats and synthesised electronica inspired by such dance music luminaries as Georgio Moroder ('I Feel Love'), Patrick Cowley, the producer behind West Coast gay dance masters Boystown Gang, Bobby O, a producer who went on to perfect the sound of The Pet Shop Boys and Ian Levine himself, who also produced Hi-NRG in the UK under the Record Shack label. The sound gave birth to a new generation of disco divas who could often be found miming or singing along to a backing track on the makeshift stages of underground gay haunts.

Producers Stock, Aitken and Waterman realised early on the potential of the pink pound and the power of the gay scene in breaking new artists. They transformed and diluted the Hi-NRG sound and mixed it with elements of Italian dance pop, creating a formula that was deemed more appealing to the masses and, soon, the charts. The Hit Factory, as they became known, effectively marketed and created gay music for mass consumption.

Kylie, and later Jason, with all their innocence and ready-made fan base, were the perfect purveyors for the Hit Factory's saccharine-coated pop and they soon became favourites with the queens, joining Bananarama, Dead or Alive, Divine, Rick Astley, Hazel Dean, Sinitta and Mel and Kim amongst others in the SAW stable. 'The Locomotion' was given the SAW treatment, recycling the original vocal that Kylie had laid down in Australia, but it was one of SAW's own songs, 'I Should Be So Lucky', that first took Kylie to the top of the English charts.

In London in 1987, Kylie recorded what is probably still her most infamous song. SAW's brand of bubblegum pop was often seen as vacuous and as irritating as a dose of crabs, but the simplicity of the lyrics and repetitious choruses provided surefire hits. Pet Shop Boy Chris Lowe commented on Kylie's first British Number One:

'I like the bit where she goes "I-I-I-I-I-I-I-I should be so lucky" and I just love the line "I should be so lucky, lucky, lucky, lucky". If that's banal, it's strength. It's just a mark of pure genius.'

The mantra of 'lucky lucky lucky' was the lyrical equivalent of water torture, based on the philosophy that if a tune and sentiment are drummed into the consciousness one will eventually succumb and go and buy the record, albeit in a braindead trance. 'I Should Be So Lucky', with the passing years, is often cited as a definitive example of a perfect pop song and it remained Kylie's bestselling single until 2001 when it was deposed by the similarly repetitious 'Can't Get You Out Of My Head' wherein the refrain 'la la la' became the 'lucky lucky lucky' for a new generation.

Stock, Aitken and Waterman and the Hit Factory weren't so far removed from my role in Neighbours: learn your lines, red light on, perform lines, no time for questions, promote the product et wilà!

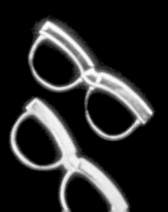

It was as a slightly more dolled-up version of Charlene that Kylie began her pop career. Pop star Charlene was just another role to play for nineteen-year-old Kylie. She had jumped straight from school onto the set of *Neighbours* and now into a recording booth.

As far as she was concerned, she was an actress and it was as an actress that she embarked on her singing career. As a child of the MTV generation she had grown up with the pop video, an art form that by 1987 was only reaching its adolescence. Prince was an early hero as was Boy George, and a Culture Club gig was the first concert she went to, plaiting her hair with ribbons like her gender-bending hero. Always at ease in front of a camera, she loved making her early videos, regarding them as an extension of acting.

As her face became more and more famous, the stylists set about her, armed with bags of huge earrings and brooches and the staple eighties fashion item, shoulder pads. Her tomboy overalls and grease monkey style gave way to the more feminine fads of high street fashion. 'The Locomotion', her second English and first Australian Number One, saw her resplendent in a red ra-ra ensemble against a backdrop of graffiti, trademark bubble perm and grin firmly in place. Later on she was also apparently an aerobics instructor, in grey sweats and headband, paying homage to Australia's then most famous export Olivia Newton-John's early eighties hit 'Let's Get Physical'.

In the 'I Should Be So Lucky' video she razzes around an apartment which now seems the epitome of eighties bad taste in interior (inferior) design, a symphony in peach melba and pastel wood veneer, with bubble curls and a black, high-waist jersey skirt and braces. The rest of the time, when she wasn't drowning in soapsuds, she pranced around in what appeared to be a cheesecloth sack. In the blue screen cutaways in which she appears against a backdrop of the most bizarre computer graphics including a magician's top hat, we get a glimpse of another character, dizzy from the noxious fumes from her hairspray. Hair straightened and wearing a black cocktail dress, the Charlene character began to give way to the actress underneath. Kylie wanted to dress up and here began the precedent of reinvention that was to become so important to her.

Her third video, for 'Got To Be Certain', another Number One on both sides of the world, showed that she had well and truly discovered the dressing-up box as she donned a number of typically colourful late eighties outfits including a hideous red bolero and radioactive green bubble skirt as she walked along Melbourne's Yarra River, marvellously accessorised with a huge Ascot-style hat which blew away, hopefully never to be seen again. On the moonlit rooftop of a Sydney skyscraper she looked slightly more chic and every inch the Australian dream as the perfect picture of health and vitality, squeezed into a stretch black boat-neck dress, white teeth gleaming, hair a perfect honey blonde and skin as gold as the coins that were piling up.

On a carousel that hadn't been oiled since Kylie was born judging by the way that it jolted every time the horses moved up and down, she wore a skin-tight red T-shirt dress with a kilt pin bearing the word 'amour' with Red or Dead platform shoes. This curious ensemble was the first sign of an English fashion influence, kilt pins with slogans winning the award for accessory of the year. Red or Dead, quintessentially English by design, was a hip new brand. Kylie was becoming international.

Her rapport with her audience, established in *Neighbours*, meant that there was no need for a formal introduction. Apart from 'The Locomotion', all her early songs were in the public mind coming from Charlene as odes to Scott the Mullet. Even 'The Locomotion' was the kind of song Charlene could have sung at a karaoke night down at the Waterhole. As a household commodity, she was ready-made. Once the word 'pop' preceded 'star' her transformation would be complete. 'I Should Be So Lucky' and 'Got To Be Certain' were songs that the public could believe were sung by Charlene and there was little attempt to separate the two personas. This was cemented by 'Especially For You', a duet with Jason Donovan. The world sighed with relief: Charlene and Scott were still very much together as they cavorted on Christmas Day on *Top of the Pops* to the delighted cheers of the audience.

Jason and I lived in each other's pockets and had little choice but to become friends early on. I think they paired our characters about three months after my arrival on the show. Friendship did indeed lead to something more and, to cut a long story short, we dated for almost three years. It was a unique and exciting time and I don't know how we would have survived without each other. We were the only ones who could appreciate what the other was going through. We were the best of friends and the line between professional and personal became ever finer. With such a crash course in the exercise of PR, we did what we thought was best and tried to keep our relationship

under wraps. This being near
impossible we tried the second best
thing and did our utmost not to
confirm or deny our romance.
This nebulous zone made us feel
safer, but I do
believe that we
instinctively
knew what
was best for
us and the
show, for
Jason and
Kylie, for
Scott and
Charlene.

Scott
&
Charlene

The soap star/pop star transition now seems commonplace but back then it was something of a novelty. The *EastEnders* stars Anita Dobson and Nick Berry mercifully spared us by giving up on the music business when both their albums flopped after the initial success of their dire debut singles, 'Anyone Can Fall In Love' and 'Every Loser Wins' respectively. The *Neighbours* stable was lucky, lucky, lucky by comparison. Jason, who Pete Waterman commented was more of a success with the teens and screaming fans at the time than Kylie, recorded at the PWL (Pete Waterman Limited) Hit Factory shortly after Kylie. He too might as well have released his singles under his character's name.

The golden couple's musical ventures were followed by Kylie's screen brother Henry with his song 'Mona' (what an apt description), bad boy Paul Robinson aka Stefan Dennis who donned studded leathers and tight jeans for a minute or two, and then the post-Kylie twins whose names escape me but who bore a remarkable resemblance to a couple of the Nolans. Natalie Imbruglia achieved almost instant pop credibility with her song 'Torn' and subsequent album, and time will tell for the latest export from the Ramsey Street stable, Holly Valance, though a surname that is the same as the frilly thing that covers up the rubbish you shove beneath the bed doesn't bode well. It has only really worked long-term for Kylie.

'Je Ne Sais Pas Pourquoi', even though it was prior to 'Especially For You', was the first Kylie video which visually implied that Charlene had dumped Scott and left Brisbane for a career in pop music. Kylie appeared fifties style, hair set in a finger wave, wearing a floral vintage dress and a cashmere bedjacket that fifteen years later would become a staple of her off-duty wardrobe.

There were no signs of her former life as a mechanic or wife to Scott Robinson as she bemoaned the fact that her date had stood her up. As she waited in the rain she wistfully dreamed of waltzing with a tall, dark hunk who was the physical opposite of Jason Donovan: dark, slick and suited, no Speedos in sight. Kylie was cutting the strings to her past and Charlene quickly became a memory. Kylie Minogue had arrived.

02

: Devil , you know

I was longing for choice
and there wasn't really
a part in the Hit Factory's
machinery or ethos for
this. Out of the studio and
confines of PWL, I started
to experiment where I
could - with image. I wanted
to develop, to experience
different things and express
myself beyond primary
colours and a shallow set
of TV answers. I was bound
to and did make mistakes,
but I believe that if you
don't allow yourself to
make mistakes then you're
not making much. I was
twenty-one and I was growing up.
My own sexual revolution.

At the premiere of her first feature film, *The Delinquents*, Kylie arrived on the arm of Australian rock star, INXS singer Michael Hutchence. The change in her appearance was remarkable. With long hair crammed under a Jean Shrimpton-style short blonde wig, she wore a minidress emblazoned with bugle-beaded noughts and crosses, designed by Australian duo Morrissey Edmiston. It caused a sensation. In the media's eyes she had stepped over a precipice and out of the confines of her little girl image and had become a woman overnight. As she and Hutchence faced the photographers, she looked every inch the star and the two of them, in co-ordinated outfits, definitely in love. His untimely and mysterious death in 1998 made him into a tragic hero, a role that unfortunately could have been tailor-made for him. For a few months back in 1989, Kylie was his *femme fatale*.

They were the Mick Jagger and Marianne Faithfull of the eighties. Marianne had been a convent schoolgirl and Jagger's various scandals had become legendary. Like Kylie, Marianne had been ready for metamorphosis and the dangerous allure of the rock'n'roll hero aided and abetted her transformation. Faithfull described him as 'always starring in an endless movie'. Hutchence, like Jagger, was an archetype: the rock'n'roll hero, an adventurer, narcissistic and with a streak of self-destruction. Live fast, die young and leave a beautiful corpse. I only met him a handful of times but he was definitely a free spirit. A law unto himself, his swarthy, earthy features made him into the Heathcliff of rock. Michael's charisma was seductive to all - he was invariably kind, courteous and open to everything, with a child's fearlessly unquenchable thirst for experience. On stage he became every inch the rock god, a Jim Morrison for our generation.

Much has been made of the so-called dangerous liaison between Michael and Kylie. Reports of mile-high escapades, of handcuffs in luggage and so forth have become media legends. The veracity of these reports will never be known: mystery, speculation and gossip are key to the creation and endurance of a mythical and legendary existence in rock. His was a life that deserves to be remembered. He was the first love of Kylie's adult life, and as with all true loves, the flame is never totally extinguished. Even now she describes feeling his presence around her, nurturing and protecting. She hopes and feels he would be proud of what she has become.

I call Kylie every morning; mornings find me at my most hyperactive and it's a good time to chat. One particular Saturday we had a show at London's GAY club at the Astoria on Charing Cross Road, run by promoter and bubblegum pop fan Jeremy Joseph and his pet pooch. We've done so many cabarets there that they have all become a bit of a blur, but I think this time Kylie was going to be carried on in a bath – the extremes you go to to make an entrance with no budget. Typically, we had left everything to the last minute and none of the dancers' or Kylie's costumes were ready. I needed to go to her place to see if her Tardis-like drawers and cupboards could rescue me from a day of traipsing around Portobello market or Bond Street. I rang Kylie because two people panicking is always better than one: it was a little early, but she always screens her calls anyway, so I figured she would answer if she was up. Kylie answered the phone sobbing... Michael had been found dead in a Sydney hotel room. She was devastated.

No words are ever enough at moments like that... I listened in stunned silence. It wasn't long ago that we had all seen Michael, his girlfriend Paula Yates and their baby at a *Top of the Pops* performance of 'Did It Again'. Paula and Michael had been so happy, delighting in baby Tiger Lily. Paula was slightly wary of Kylie: most women would be edgy if their boyfriend's ex was Kylie, but there was no bad feeling. Kylie had never lost anyone before. Death seems incomprehensible when you are young. Michael had a self-destructive streak yet he had seemed immortal. Stars so often seem invincible, larger than life, their lives created, catalogued and somehow protected through the bold headlines of the tabloid front pages. Media stars seem permanent because of the indelible record of the TV or movie screen. When death comes, especially to those who are no longer a fixture of our daily lives, it seems surreal.

Kylie felt her world had crumbled under her feet. She and flatmate Nikki, also a close friend of Michael, didn't leave the house all day, trying to confront the reality of it, reminiscing about their times with this enigmatic man and finding some comfort in shared grief. Michael, like Kylie, had that rare quality of being able to make anyone feel special, be it a fan, a friend or colleague. He saw everyone as a new experience in life's extraordinary tapestry, and his presence and generosity of spirit enabled everyone, no matter how famous they may or may not have been, to feel they had something unique to offer.

M+K Sep '90 LA

Kylie didn't cancel that night. When smitten by a virus years later on the first dates of her Fever tour she croaked that 'cancel' was not a word in her vocabulary. But if ever there was a moment that epitomised her philosophy that the show must go on, it was never more poignantly expressed than on the day of Michael Hutchence's death. Kylie felt humbled by death. She felt that to cancel a show in front of her ever-faithful gay audience was a cop-out. I remember her saying clearly on the phone that she had never faced death until now, but she thought she owed it to a community that had been ravaged by loss from the AIDS epidemic to perform that night.

How we deal with death is at least as important as how we deal with life. The show was a strain. Kylie tried to hold it together during hair and make-up prep at home but the pain and loss in her eyes couldn't be concealed by any amount of make-up and it all seemed slightly superfluous. In true Brit fashion, her team carried on as if nothing had happened, repeatedly putting the kettle on and drinking copious amounts of tea. She held together well for the show, but when Jeremy Joseph presented her with a bouquet of flowers that was nearly the same size as her and he and the audience expressed their gratitude and sympathy, the flood gates opened and she fled from the building in tears.

Michael's funeral was a touching and tragic tribute to one of Australia's heroes. The tabloids the next day were not so much preoccupied by the funeral as by the number of ex-girlfriends amongst the mourners. That he left such beauty behind seemed an apt tribute to a man whom they perceived as Byronic. The papers published a photograph of a devastated Minogue, veil failing to conceal her anguish. It was one of those rare moments when the paparazzi capture a moment and person so perfectly. Kylie looked glamorous, beautiful, fragile and vulnerable, with a grace and dignity that had become increasingly rare in the nineties world of celebrity, the image capturing her essence as no staged session ever could.

That photo was taken as we were walking out of the church. It was an incredibly hot day in Sydney with the sun blazing down, but at the end of the service, in true Byronic fashion, clouds came rolling in and we could hear the thunder from inside. Rain started to pour down and it was the final straw in what had been an intensely emotional day for everyone. Michael had been a 'first' for me in so many ways and I remember thinking, this is just typical that he would teach me about the pain and strength and worldliness that come with loving someone. He was always teaching me and that was an integral part of our relationship.

I was twenty-one and metaphorically he took my blinkers off and opened my eyes to a bigger world. More intriguing, exciting, dangerous, sexy, beautiful and poetic. He told me he was overwhelmed by my innocence and thirst for experience, seeing me mature in front of his eyes.

As Faithfull had described Jagger, Michael had also lived his life like a movie. Like any good movie, there had been sex, drugs, rock'n'roll, laughter, tears, love, loss and beauty, and like any good movie, Michael will be for ever remembered.

his image, both in terms of his media image and his personal style. Kylie learned from him the power of sexuality and he ignited a spark deep within. She had never really enjoyed her body let alone displayed it in videos or photographs. Suddenly the clothes came off as she revelled in being a sexy twenty-one-year-old. She was becoming a woman. Before Hutchence, she was demure and coy, as if she didn't really possess a sex life or sexuality. Ironically, in the eyes of many, her innocence had given her a sexuality in itself - if she had but known it. Now the girl-next-door was redecorating and her sexuality became more obvious. She transformed into a fully-fledged siren.

The old Kylie and all the ra-ra skirts, big hats and brooches literally went up in smoke in the video for 'Better The Devil You Know'. Her hair was straightened and she burned with a new vibrancy, bra strap slipping from her shoulder as she cavorted away. It came as a surprise to some that she even wore a bra, but the strap dropping onto her arm proved that she was well versed in the natural art of female seduction. The dancers around her suddenly became sexual stereotypes as the inane Steps lookalikes from her previous videos were booted and replaced with a posse of black men, gyrating wildly in the background. This pivotal video was also notable as the first celluloid appearance of the hot pants which have become Kylie's trademark. Kylie was fast evolving.

Hair blowing with wind machine on full power, arms raised above her head and lifted by a black man, his hands clearly defined against her pale flesh, it was apparent that she was well underway on the course of what she described as her own 'sexual revolution'. The fact that the love interest dancer in the video was black is significant: the sexualising of the black male and implied interracial relationship were clearly pushing boundaries in Kylie's own way. This wouldn't have been worthy of comment had not her previous videos been so twee and asexual by comparison. Earlier male dancers had been mere smiling twirlies who could have doubled as children's TV presenters. Now they were 'real' men endowed with strong muscular silhouettes.

The song also featured a more mature sound, a more polished production and a vocal that was less layered than before. The track transferred well onto the dance-floor and heralded a long reign for Kylie as the new queen of disco... a pop princess. Her coronation was celebrated in 'Step Back In Time', shot in downtown LA and directed by Nick Egan in a brilliant homage to the music and dance moves of the era that created disco, the seventies.

055-091

'Glamour is defined as alluring charm or fascination, often based on illusion that transforms or glorifies a person or thing.'
Larry Carr

Glamour, as a concept, is an invention of the early twentieth century and the golden age of Hollywood. Screen goddesses were created with the birth of silent black-and-white cinema and continued through the 'talkies' and the advent of colour. Starlets were manufactured by the all-powerful studio moguls to promote the idea of fledgling actresses attaining divine status. Marlene Dietrich, Joan Crawford, Greta Garbo, Gloria Swanson, Marilyn Monroe, Brigitte Bardot, Gina Lollobrigida et al. all became synonymous with glamour, their air-brushed faces benchmarks of immortal beauty. But their images were also illusions, flawless masks shot through a vaselined lens which distorted truth and nature. John Updike once said that 'fame is a mask that eats away at the face'.

Images and photographs of these early starlets were painstakingly retouched and manipulated by hand, the subtle changes often etched onto the actual negative itself. The retoucher's hand created an ideal, as any unforgivable physical imperfection – too big a nose, too hairy an eyebrow, too thin a lip – was eradicated, an engineered interpretation of an imperfect subject. The studios manipulated their starlets so that they became durable icons, visions of unreal loveliness, at once ageless and immortal. These photographic technicians were the real unsung heroes of Hollywood, creating a standard of beauty that will never again be achieved.

Kylie, having been groomed first in the slightly less glamorous TV studios of Melbourne in the fine arts of performance and posing, knew all this. At this pivotal moment in her life she experimented with ways in which a glamorous image could be constructed from sources around her. The camera loved her and she loved it back, exploring and projecting her most seductive angles. She'd learned quickly that the display of her body could say as much as the features of her face. The transition of her image had taken on an almost drag aspect as, hurtling towards becoming a modern screen goddess, she explored the extremes of artificial femininity. She became a blank canvas for her own explorations and experimentation, as her size eight, five-foot-one body became both artist and canvas, stylist and model, subject and object.

Musically she remained within the confines of the Hit Factory although her vocal style was becoming increasingly honed into a distinctive, iconic pop voice. The productions remained formulaic but created a series of top ten hits which further expanded a loyal fan base.

Michael taught me about the ego jacket that you put on before you go out on stage. You transform, you become something else, a combination of the person you are and the person people want you to be. It's a harmonious coming together of person and projection.

The video 'What Do I Have To Do?' evoked the glamorous images of the starlets of Hollywood's heyday. Kylie's eyebrows were heavily pencilled and lips more clearly defined in the manner of a screen goddess. Her looks became increasingly dramatic, almost to the point of caricature. Liz Taylor, Joan Collins and Brigitte Bardot were all honoured as London's wig stores were plundered and stylist David Thomas was dispatched to Paris to raid the showrooms of Azzedine Alaia and Thierry Mugler, designers who played with a cinched high-waisted, long-legged, sculpted form of fantasy woman.

Both designers approached the female form with an architectural philosophy, their genius pattern-cutting defining the power silhouette of the late eighties/early nineties woman. It was the era of the supermodel and glamour was experiencing a long overdue comeback.

When I spoke with the director David Trojan on the phone, he asked me what style I was into. That was easy: 'Italian Vogue'. There was a particular issue I had in mind that was bulging with black and white photographs of impossibly beautiful and glamorous women. He knew it & was in love with it too, so we made a video where I looked like as many screen icons as possible in three and a half minutes. Our plagiarism was unapologetic and I happily stepped into a predetermined mould of 'sexy' and had fun. With that much artifice it was easy not to take it too seriously.

Kylie had well and truly discovered the dressing-up box. She pouted, flirted and flaunted her new drag elegance, teetering on her new staple item, stilettos. From that point on, like Dolly Parton, she was never without them.

or less the same when they are out
buying a pint of milk. In my performance
you see a facet, part of my character
and personality. When you're talking
about clothes and style in reference
to a media representation, dressing up
is another type of performance. In
this busy world, image can say a lot
in a moment. For this reason it's
essential in what I do.

The most successful results of
Kylie's romance with the camera
are the photographs that capture
her spirit; they exude glamour,
convey silent conversation,
whisper intimacy. They mesmerise
and smoulder. But there is
another characteristic which is
also evident in old Hollywood
photographs of studio starlets
and movie icons: vulnerability.
Bert Stern, a photographer famous
for his *Last Sitting* photographs
of Marilyn Monroe, remarked on
the similarities between Monroe
and Minogue, which included
fragility and sensuality, a
juxtaposition of erotic power and
vulnerability. Never has this
been more succinctly captured
than in Minogue's long-time
collaborations with close friend
and photographer Katerina Jebb.

Kylie met Kat in Paris in
1991, after her relationship with
Michael ended with a phone-call.
Heartbroken, Kylie had sought
refuge and escape in the
melancholic romanticism of the
city, away from the constant
glare of London's paparazzi. She
didn't want to be reminded of
anything to do with him. Kylie
travelled to Paris with just two
phone numbers in her pocket of
people she had recently met. She
went for dinner at one of these
friends' flats and the person
that greeted her at the door of
the *seizième* apartment was Kat.
From that moment on they became
very close.

Kat photographed Kylie
constantly, and always from her
unique and very feminine
perspective. Kat wanted to see
the real Kylie. She hated the
drag queen look, rubbing off
Kylie's heavily drawn eyebrows
and covering her cheeks with only
a hint of rouge to give her an
English rose look. With Kat's
help and influence as friend and
photographer, Kylie peeled away
the layers of her public image,
and began to develop her own
personality and character. If her
relationship with Michael had
been her period of rebellion, the
painful months that followed the
split were her coming-of-age.
Kat's influence on Kylie was
huge.

Working with Kat was a dream ♡♡. She was my best friend and I truly admired her talent. There was also none of the pressure associated with other shoots. We could do what we wanted, just for our own pleasure. It was usually just me, Kat and the camera. We would do my hair and make-up, on occasion we hired one or two lights, which we would both have to lug around. We had alter ego characters. She was the salubrious 'Ricardo of London - Photographer to the Stars', and I was 'Tony' his assistant, who worked evenings as a singer in dodgy cabaret clubs.

In the guise of their alter egos, Ricardo of London would loom over assistant Tony, whispering under his breath, 'Come over here and let me see how you're hung.'

Kat shaped the woman that Kylie is today, influencing her style possibly more than any other individual. Their working relationship is perhaps best compared to the one Eve Arnold and Marilyn Monroe enjoyed. Kat's technique was not so much voyeurism as reportage, capturing Kylie's *joie de vivre* – the reality and not the artifice surrounding her friend.

Her staged photos present a Kylie that is quintessentially feminine, vulnerable and glamorous. She is girlie, flirtatious, beautiful, natural and real. She plays and flirts with the archetypes of femininity, of the Playboy bunny, of the Vargas girl, of the Hollywood damsel in distress, of the Lolita, of the single girl. Kat suffered a serious road accident, leaving her arm partially paralysed, and causing a great deal of constant pain. There is often a darkness latent within the images, a result of this pain, and of Kat's own very black sense of humour. They also possess a very English quality. Kat preferred thrift store antiques to the latest fashions. Consequently her images, that were not subject to the ever-changing whims of the catwalk and fashion photography, are timeless.

Kat provided Kylie with a 'lifetime's reportage', and they are still close and often work together to this day.

Kat was living with Kylie in London when I first met Kylie. I remember the first time I went to their apartment and Kat entered the room, eyeing me suspiciously, a potential invader of their private world. I was amazed at the number of photo sessions that the two had undertaken, the results of which lie in Kat's many suitcases now lying in hiding in various locations all over the globe. They were planning one of their shoots, Kylie inspired by a video of Blondie performing live, and that particular shoot remains one of my favourites.

I wasn't allowed to attend that shoot, but I supplied the clothes for it. They were a veritable pot-pourri of pop trivia. The stained Marilyn Monroe T-shirt I unearthed originally belonged to Terri Toy, a transsexual who was one of Andy Warhol's later superstars, hanging around the Factory in the early eighties. Terri modelled herself on ill-fated superstar Edie Sedgwick, of the film *Ciao! Manhattan,* and Penelope Tree, the famous seventies muse and model for designer Stephen Sprouse. It had found its way from Ms Toy to New York stylist 'sticky' Vicky Bartlett, who had then given it to Murray Blewett, whom I was assisting at Vivienne Westwood and living with at the time.

Murray also hoarded many of Vivienne's early Seditionaries clothes sold in her King's Road boutique in 1977. Vivienne, in Gene Krell's words, was 'punk's prototype and greatest showpiece... every mother's nightmare and voice of a generation'. It seemed ironic to dip Kylie into the ethos of punk, and her 'genocide peroxide' attitude in the images reveals the defiance of rebellion, and a harder, self-assured sexuality. Another T-shirt she wore in the shoot features sexually explicit handwritten text and two zips covering the breasts, and was a Seditionaries original titled 'She groaned'. Another featured the famous 'tit' print.

I gave her tiny size three silver and perspex mules to wear, which were said to have belonged to Jordan, Sex's shop assistant around 1974 and member of a group of punk originators that included singer Siouxsie Soux and notorious club promoter Philip Salon, and that became known as the Bromley Contingent. The vintage was mixed with micro minis courtesy of Vivienne's latest collection at the time, Anglomania, an updated and glamorised vision of punk mixed with sumptuous tartans, exquisite gold tulle and Vivienne's famous platform court shoes. Coincidentally, it was the Paris show *Anglomania* in which Naomi Campbell tumbled over her blue mock croc elevated courts.

Kat opened my eyes to the world of photography and the world in general. She nurtured me. I was destined to meet her at that time.

Our holiday in Turkey, which of course ended up as a photo shoot.

I had always been fascinated by clothes and the drag of the pop star. My earliest memory of this obsession goes back to October 1982. It was a freezing autumn evening and I was on the way home from my weekly cub scout meeting. I hated every minute of the cubs, not least because it was on the same night as the new *Fame* TV show. Every week I had to be dragged there, virtually kicking and screaming. All I learned from the whole hideous experience was how to make a cup of tea. And why one has to be educated in the art of tying knots I will never know. To this day I can't even knot a piece of threaded cotton. Kylie has to do that for me.

This particular Thursday I was even more distressed than usual after missing the latest instalment of the exploits of those kids from the New York School of Performing Arts, as I had developed a raging adolescent crush on Danny, the wannabe stand-up comic, and in my imagination we were in the throes of a torrid affair. Cubs was screwing up my whole life. As my dad drove me home after a gruelling session in which we had attempted to cook sausages over a campfire (camp being the appropriate word), he was fulminating about the singer with a new Number One single on *Top of the Pops*. 'I don't know what it was,' he said, 'if it was a boy or a girl...' My dad thought whatever it was prancing on that stage had been pretty. It was Boy George. I was entranced the first time I saw him on *Swap Shop*, I think, the following Saturday morning. George opened up a whole new world for me, away from my home in leafy Cheshire. It wasn't so much the music, though I played it all the time, but more the way he looked. As yet unaware of David Bowie or Marc Bolan or the glam rock explosion which had years earlier influenced George and the club scene from which he had emerged, I was nonetheless fascinated by this man who wore make-up and smocks. I began to learn about George and his background, submerging myself in all the fanzines, the annuals, books and, of course, the records.

In the next three years, as the world's most photographed person after Princess Diana, from 'Do You Really Want To Hurt Me?' to 'The War Song', George turned from a young asexual pantomime dame into an almost fully fledged tranny, becoming the first man to grace the covers of *Cosmopolitan* and *Woman's Own*. By the time he was all but crucified in the press following the revelations about his heroin addiction, I was a devoted fan, bunking off school art trips to London to go and sit on his doorstep, dressed head to toe in Boy get-up, braces wrapped around me, safety pins everywhere and eyebrows to die for. I would spend all my clothing allowance on the latest fabulous range of Rouge Extreme lipsticks from Chanel. The lady behind the Chanel counter at Kendal's in Manchester became my friend, often slipping me free make-up samples which I would smear all over my face in McDonald's loos, subsequently removing it in the train toilets on the way home.

My gran lived at the top of my road and trying to escape to Manchester yet avoiding her eagle-eyed watch of the comings and goings of Orchard Green was nearly impossible. Hiding my clothes was one thing but the make-up was too much to inflict on the residents of Alderley Edge, most of whom were over seventy, and many of them had known me since I was a baby. My penchant for high-quality cosmetics almost got me well and truly busted once as I spent the afternoon with the freak posse from school, loitering in Altrincham shopping precinct. Resplendent in red bondage trousers, matching jacket and ever-present Boy cap, I was sporting the latest lippy in Chanel's range, Ruby. I nearly had a coronary as I clocked my mum and gran doing a spot of shopping and I rubbed at my lips maniacally, trying to remove the red and avoid being grounded. Chanel lived up to its reputation as the *crème de la crème* of *maquillage* and the lipstick wouldn't budge no matter how hard I rubbed. I must have looked like Ronald McDonald by the time my mum and gran caught up with me, but fortunately for me Gran had developed cataracts and didn't notice.

Pop stars as idols are omnipotent and can do no wrong in the eyes of their disciples. George as a role model shaped and moulded my personality, style (or lack of), and interests for life. If it weren't for him, I wouldn't even like to think what I would be doing today. His sexuality and uncompromisingly big gob, and the fact that he was screwing his straight drummer, exemplified the positive influential power that a pop star could have on an audience and he saved me a great deal of anguish in my youth; thanks to him I never even questioned the right or wrong of fancying boys at school.

Pop stars should entertain, inspire, educate, and provide escape. I believe their influence as role models is a vital function of their work. I've always been drawn to outspoken pop stars such as Madonna and Eminem but you can often say a lot more by manipulating an image in a photograph or video, or dressing something up, than you can with words. Image is an expression and a tool. It makes me sad to see the current state of today's cabbage patch of pop stars and I'm glad to have grown up at a time when pop was such a bitchy, vibrant and colourful circus.

Pop has been demystified even more by reality TV shows such as *Popstars*, the final death throes of a genre that has become increasingly mundane and grey. Illusion is vital if the 'normal' is to morph mysteriously into star magic but all the tricks are laid bare for all to see. Compulsive viewing it may be, but kids need a little more from pop than a Versace suit and a cover of an old chestnut. The whole appeal of pop stars is that they aren't 'normal' and the widespread normalising of pop is depressing. The archetype of the everyday hero/heroine has always been there, be it in the form of The Osmonds, Sean and David Cassidy, Ronan Keating or Kylie early in her career, but a hunger to evolve and grow seems to be absent in many of today's performers. Accessibility has become the norm and the charts are filled these days with armies of puppets all singing the same old songs and all wearing the same old thing.

The cogs and bolts of manufactured pop's machinery displayed so openly in the Hit Factory in the eighties and early nineties left a legacy of blandness. Today the PR machines and pulp pop industry have perhaps stifled the personalities of many artists as the puppet masters prefer their performers to be blank canvases. Manufactured pop has produced its giants in recent years – think of The Spice Girls and Take That – but there is a definite trend towards the bland. There are some welcome exceptions: Will Young's outing by the tabloids made him immediately far more interesting than his rival Gareth Gates, and the fact that Will isn't a screaming queen like John Inman, Julian Clary or Graham Norton contributes to a much broader interpretation of the gay spectrum than what had often pertained before. The fact that Will doesn't seem remotely bothered, not even considering his sexuality to be a relevant ingredient in the making of his pop career, is a step forward, not only in terms of his function as an appropriate role model but also in terms of our times' increasing need to generate more rounded, three-dimensional performers. No scandal followed the revelation and it didn't affect his record sales or public image either. A definite turnaround from years ago when homosexuality was considered a character defect. He still sings songs about girls though, but give him time...

Jason Donovan's pop career went right down the dumper when he sued *The Face* ten years earlier for implying he was gay. He sued to set a precedent and won. Jason was a 'gay straight' from the start, a heterosexual man who sported a groomed look – just as David Beckham does today – but he failed to realise the potential power this gave him. Will Young, on the other hand, is a 'straight gay', benefiting from the best of all worlds.

I was more or less adopted by my gay audience. In fact, I was possibly the last to know. In the early 1990's, 'The Albury' on Sydney's Oxford Street hosted a 'Kylie' night every Sunday. This was the first time I had heard of a 'Kylie Drag Show'. I don't like to analyse our relationship too much as it is what it is and it's wonderful, but I think they related to my initial struggle to be accepted as myself and then to survive. Later still my wrestles with contradiction. Not to mention my penchant for all things pink and showgirl...

Kylie had learned much from her manufactured roots, her feet firmly on the ground with an astute understanding of the varied elements and demographics that made up her audience. To succeed and then achieve longevity, she knew she had to embrace the nature and power of image. Styling, make-up and hair combine to create a persona and can embellish and extend the personality of the performer, while clothes also create iconic images.

Madonna's ethos is immortalised by her collaborations with Jean-Paul Gaultier, the conical bras and gold corset being definitive examples of such iconography in pop. The image of Madonna in a man's suit, monocle in place, and pink salmon bra bursting through the pin-stripe fabric said every necessary thing about Madonna at the time. Words would have been superfluous. 'One should either be a work of art or wear a work of art,' wrote Oscar Wilde in *Phrases and Philosophies for the Use of the Young*. Image can provide a mask, concealing true nature and creating a perfected and fantastic illusion.

Kylie's drag queen impersonation in 'What Do I Have To Do?' leapt out from the screen at me and in those three and a half minutes of celluloid hi-camp, her whole future and its infinite diversity of possibilities opened up in my mind's eye. The shot where she is ironing, dressed in a Mugler version of a French maid's outfit, hurling the iron back and forth with more make-up on than Boy George, Marilyn and Pete Burns put together, remains my all-time favourite image of her, glamorising the most mundane of household chores. Not a fraction of an inch of those eyebrows melted as the steam rose from the fifties iron and from that moment I became a Kylie fan.

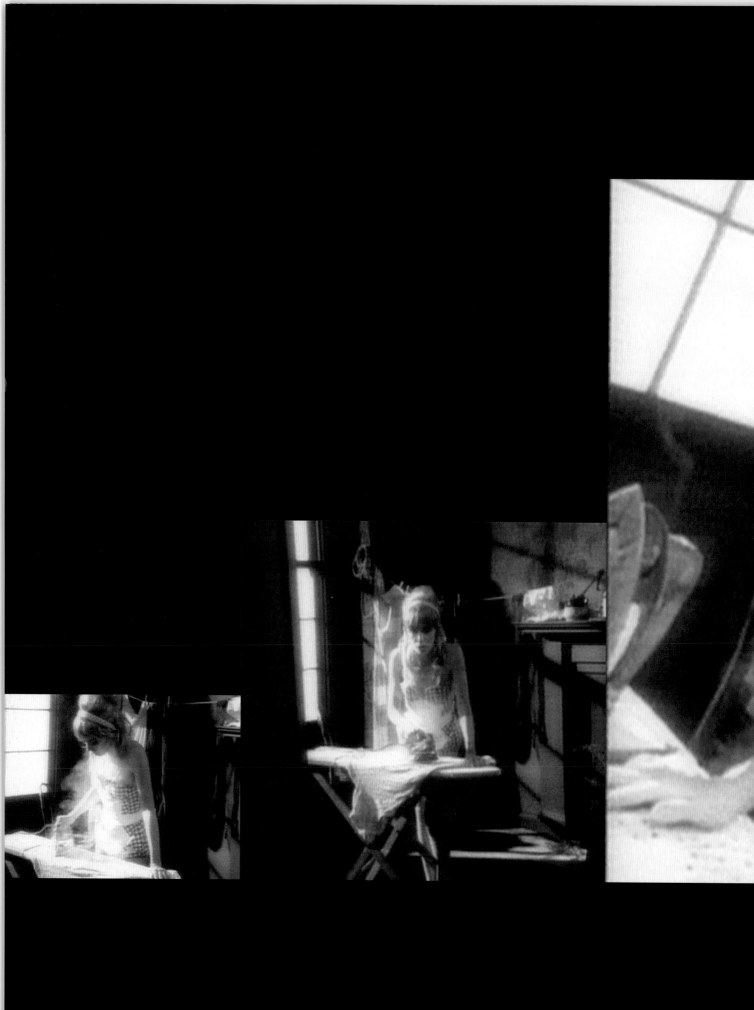

I never assumed that was how she looked when she ironed her tiny G-strings, but it was the fantasy element, the escapist dream of this pocket Bardot housemaid that hit me as hard as if she had belted me around the face with one of her Manolos. I loved every second of the video and the song. The imaginary fusion of Joan Collins meets Liz Taylor with a tattooed panther on her back perfectly expressed the playful seduction, flirtatious charm, and kitsch glamour of the girl that I was soon to meet. With that video, she unwittingly cornered every conceivable member of a pop audience: her gay fans admired the drag sensibility, her little girl fans dived into their mothers' make-up bags, her straight male fans wanted to bend her over the ironing board, and older girls wanted to nip down to the wig shop and reinvent themselves.

The trend continued in the video for 'Shocked', which featured Kylie in a number of guises. One minute she is dressed in pink gingham with her hair in bunches, the next in leather hot pants and bra over a mesh catsuit, hair getting bigger and bigger, then she is shimmying in a pink ostrich skirt, and finally she appears in an oversized man's suit, shirt and tie, setting off her post-coitally knotted hair. This period witnessed the birth of the kitsch thread which has weaved through her career in performance, photographs and video ever since. Captured in a Paris photo session by Ellen Von Unwerth, the images are definitive examples of her unique brand of 'sweet kitsch'. The period is seen by her fans as the pinnacle of her Stock, Aitken and Waterman years. Suddenly Kylie was cool. She began appearing not just in the *Smash Hits* and pop publications of the time, but her increasingly made-up visage began to grace the cover of the world's style magazines and Kylie now commanded the attention of the planet's best photographers.

Selecting her visual biographers from the world of fashion, she knew they would give her a look and style that was contemporary yet timeless. *Tatler* had featured her as a cover girl a couple of years before with what appeared to be a dead crow on her head, photographed by Michael Roberts, but now her cool status was celebrated by style bibles such as *The Face* and *i-D*. Kylie was clearly enjoying experimenting with her image and her dalliances with the dressing-up box and her unique DIY glamour won her a legion of new fans.

What ARE you talking about !?

It's hysterical. I hear some astonishing stories and rumours about me from that time that are so absurd I can only laugh. It's true I was immersing myself in clubland culture and would dance among other places, in my slashed John Galliano skirt,

Suddenly what she wore mattered and was talked about. Kylie was a star. London's thriving subcultural life was an increasing influence and she became a regular fixture in the clubs of the time. Legends abound in clubland of her dancing the night away with a huge entourage, and *that* rumour of her getting her foot stuck in a toilet in Subterania, a club in Ladbroke Grove, still does the rounds today.

until the place closed. It has more than just going down to the local disco. I felt that I lived in London. I was a part of it and being heavily influenced by the music and fashion coming from it. DJ's, designers, choreographers, stylish all assumed a new importance and, rather than seeming unattainable as they once did, they were before me.

Media interest by now was intense. Photographers, stylists and fashion designers joined her legions of fans as she worked and mingled with the likes of John Galliano, Rifat Ozbek, Jean-Paul Gaultier, photographer Marc Le Bon and jewellery designer and stylist Judy Blame, all of whom became integral to the peddling of the new cool Kylie. For a cover of *The Face*, Andrew MacPherson photographed her curling her glued-on lashes, with the headline 'Kylie Remade'. Galliano later went on to design the costumes for her Rhythm Of Love tour in 1991, a tour that attracted comment about its visual similarities to Madonna's Blonde Ambition a year earlier.

aspirational to the middle, or prop ... of
fashion, meant that I wasn't immune
to the trends she created. I admire
Madonna greatly and of course was
thrilled to have my name plastered
over her chest years later at the MTV
Awards. I thought it was clever...
bestowing her seal of approval as the
'Queen of Pop' upon the new wave of 'Pop
Princesses.' I couldn't have asked for
a better advertisement! But this world
is big enough for all of us. Competition
allows us to thrive, to work harder
and develop.

Comparisons with Madonna were
inevitable, but - garters,
fishnets and girdles aside -
totally inappropriate, the two
sharing only a chameleon instinct
for reinvention. Galliano also

Her love of all things London
continued as her videos began to
feature personalities and male
models instantly recognisable
from the style mags and the
London club scene. Subterania
doorgirl Davina McCall, now a TV
presenter, and photographer Mario
Sorrenti featured alongside Kylie
and her new friends in the clip
for 'Word Is Out'.

By this time I had become
aware of the people behind the
scenes that actually created
these images, the photographers,
video directors and stylists. Boy
George at the time was
collaborating with Judy Blame,
who had also worked with Kylie
and was a friend of a friend of a
friend. Judy was contributing
fashion editor of *i-D* magazine
and remains a visionary in his
avant-garde approach to fashion
and styling. As a result of this
tentative connection we met in
London. Judy took me to a small
nightclub in Paddington, a dingy
hole of a place that mixed music
and short films projected on its
walls. The club was filled with
faces I recognised from my
suburban perusal of the style
mags and in a corner, canoodling
with her then boyfriend, was
Kylie.

THE FACE

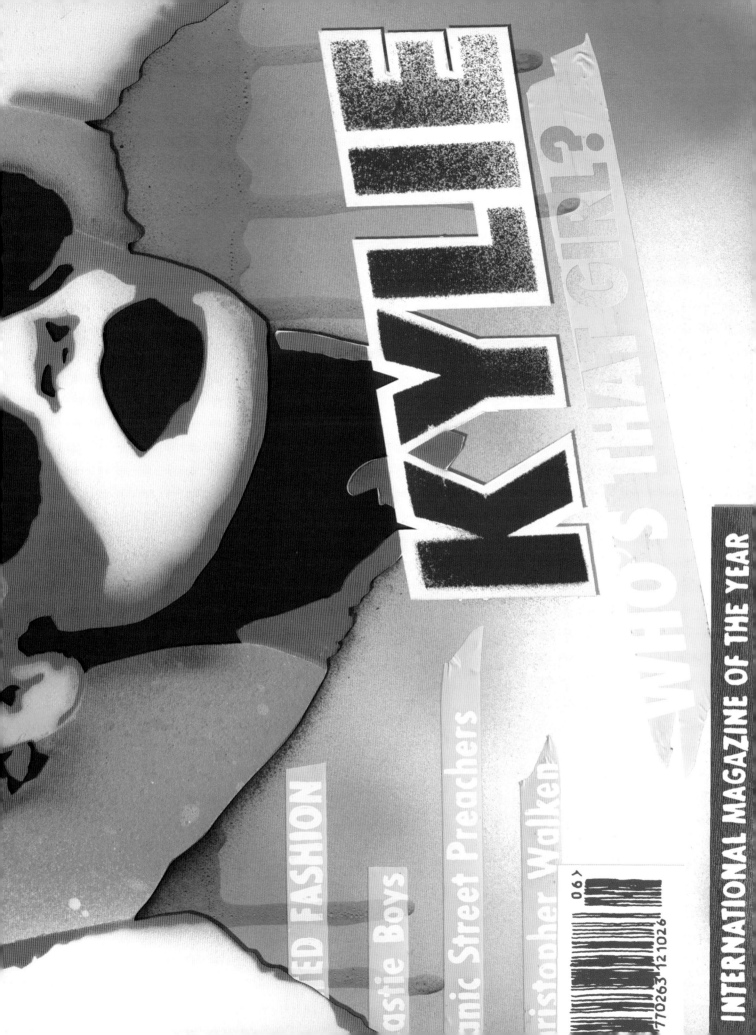

THE FACE

KYLIE

WHO'S THAT GIRL?

INTERNATIONAL MAGAZINE OF THE YEAR

ED FASHION

astie Boys

anic Street Preachers

ristopher Walken

06

9 770263 121026

Boredom is my enemy!.
Change is as natural to me as breathing.

Back in the eighties and early nineties, the institutions of music production tended to keep recording artists in their respective boxes. It was difficult for singers to explore genres of popular music other than the style with which they were associated. If you were a rock or so-called serious singer, it was considered a sell-out to record something in a pop or dance style and vice versa. To regard pop as an art form then was considered uncool. Many singers strove to escape from vacuous pop bracketing and move towards more serious music. Few revelled in pop for pop's sake.

It is only the benefit of passing years and hindsight that elevates the banal into the territory of the fabulous and cool. Pop was judged to be the lowest of the low in the 'cool' stakes, due in the most part to SAW's manufactured pop legacy.

Over the past fifteen years, Madonna and Kylie are the only female singers who have achieved longevity in pop, expanding and manipulating the genre's definition, and embracing and exploring other types of music – guitar, indie, electro or dance – whilst maintaining loyalty to a pure pop philosophy. A great or even just good pop song transcends musical genres, as exemplified by The Beatles' work. A Beatles song can be placed over a funk track, a house track or a soul track and still hold its identity as a slice of pop. A pure pop song is the harmonious unification of often simple melody and lyric. Madonna and Kylie made it cool to like pop again.

In any creative field it is impossible to please everybody. I have had my share of criticism and although it does hurt, I think it has made me stronger. I have a sensitive nature but a strong constitution and I am quietly very resilient. I'm very demanding of myself, which can exasperate friends, but it means I can usually find a challenge to immerse myself in.

As a purveyor of pop, Kylie has received more than her fair share of knocks from both the music industry and the general public yet she has, much to the annoyance of some more 'serious' artist detractors, proved that behind the pin-up exterior, she is an adept and successful songwriter. Amongst the myriad criticisms levelled at her, she is still sometimes classified as a one-dimensional performer or talent:

'I have a massive problem with her because she epitomises the acceptable role. She makes records for men. Loads of blokes like the Manic Street Preachers and Bobby Gillespie [of Primal Scream] go on about her being a great pop star, but can you remember the words? It's a shame she gets so much credibility when there are so many women worth a hundred times that; it annoys me that Sinead O'Connor has a great voice but people slag her off. As a woman going on stage you have to have a degree of responsibility. It's war... you shouldn't stick up for Kylie, she should be fought at every turn.'

This opinion, offered by indie singer Miki Berenyi from the group Lush, has been advanced more than once by critics. It clearly misses the point of Kylie. She does not make 'records for men', as any study of the demographics of her audience would reveal; a large part of it has always been female. If anything, the smallest segment of her audience is the adult male, who like the look but are notoriously slow to part with cash to buy records. They aren't likely to buy pop records anyway, preferring the pub rock of such lad icons as Oasis, Travis and Coldplay. Kylie revels in being a girl and girlie and whilst those lads may stick her image on their walls, relatively few buy her records.

The second point to refute in this argument is that ninety-nine per cent of people in this country *could* recite the lyrics of at least one Kylie song, be it 'I Should Be So Lucky', 'Better The Devil You Know', or 'Can't Get You Out Of My Head'. Pop music is the musical soundtrack to all our lives, musical wallpaper for our day-to-day existence. Often we hum or sing a tune that we have heard either in a shop, in the car, on the radio or on the TV, regardless of whether or not we like it. Such is pop's power.

Kylie's blend of pop operates on both subconscious and conscious levels. Being a pop star is often considered to be at odds with being a musician. Kylie replies that she is not a musician, preferring the term 'performer' to describe her career and talent. The age-old, stereotypical contest between beauty and talent seems to cause many people problems with her.

While much has been made of her looks, there is a quiet revolution going on underneath the surface. This lady is a formidable talent, who displayed early in her career an understanding of the mechanics of the music industry. She has perfected her image and enjoys the process while all the while developing a near perfect pop voice. Kylie has proved that she wasn't and isn't an image stereotype. Focus on her image and her pin-up status has often detracted from the fact that beneath the gloss there is a performer who has endured in a highly competitive arena for more than fifteen years. It is too easy to dismiss her as pretty but mindless and talentless. Her unassuming girl-next-door accessibility also detracts from the fact that underneath all that candy icing there is a keen business acumen and understanding of her profession.

Julie Burchill captured
Kylie's ethos of defiance:

'"I would rather be a tiny bit
vulgar than be boring -
especially to myself," the great
architect Sir Clough Williams-
Ellis once said, and in Kylie's
butterfly life we see this same
fear of dreariness which informs
all great modern careers. Her
show-boating is more sincere than
Bono's sighs, her carpet-bagging
far more creative than Oasis'
endless water-treading, and how
sad the men look who complain
"she doesn't write her own
songs." But Pavlova never
choreographed her own ballets,
and Garbo never wrote her own
scripts. The principle remains
the same; it's that lumpen,
literal-minded masculine ethos
again, insisting that everything
must be "natural" and nothing
must be a production. But, as
Oscar Wilde pointed out, being
natural is the biggest pose of
all...'

It was commonplace around ten
years ago to agree that Kylie was
a puppet. Her genius is that,
although her success is
undoubtedly due to collaboration
with others, it is she and her
management who astutely choose
the puppet masters. Such are her
sunshine presence, her smiling
personality and her diminutive
stature that suited men generally
temporarily forget the old adage
about the female of the species
being deadlier than the male, and
are often quick to succumb to her
power when confronted by it. Such
men may think they are in control
but when Kylie enters the room
any impartial observer would see
that there is only one person
really pulling the strings. And
whoever may be portrayed as
pulling Kylie's puppet strings,
it's best to remember that Kylie
chose them in the first place.
    Her decision to leave SAW was
indicative of this.

The 'Hit Factory'
was aptly named.
Their system is one truly
to be admired & I now
understand why they
weren't so keen to indulge
some of my fancies.
'If it aint broke.....'
It was a tight and
skilful operation.
A part of
POP HISTORY.

A brief renaissance in her later PWL years, the triptych 'Better The Devil You Know', 'What Do I Have To Do?' and 'Shocked' had resurrected the tried and tested formula, but after 'Shocked' the songs reverted to the more formulaic tunes of old. Kylie tried her best to inject life into 'Word Is Out', and succeeded with 'Gimme Just A Little More Time', but the songs wore hooves, and Kylie, expressing all her creative frustrations with her image, took the hi-camp glamour of 'What Do I Have To Do?' and 'Shocked' to extremes of butch/femme drag in 'Word Is Out', with hair set in demi-wave, tons of black eyeliner and a split Galliano skirt and bustier ensemble, revealing a stockinged leg. In 'Finer Feelings' she maintained her Hollywood chic in a gorgeous slice of black-and-white romanticism, based in a Paris evocative of the romance of the city captured by photographers Brassaï and Doisneau.

Her last two singles from the Hit Factory, 'What Kind Of Fool' and 'Celebration', could have been recorded three years earlier, showing no signs of musical direction or development. Although signed for just three albums, Kylie recorded four with the Hit Factory but by the time of *Let's Get To It*, her final album on the label, the magic was gone and the record sank quickly.

Kylie had already proved that she could control and manipulate her image, but now that she felt she had more to offer musically, she had gone as far as she could with PWL. And so she entered the deConstruction fold in 1993, a small independent dance label that, shortly after her signing, became a subsidiary of music giant BMG. Pete Hadfield, one of deConstruction's A&R team, remembers:

'There was this great misconception... she was far from a puppet in any meeting I had with her... She's a very driven individual, very creative, very aware of imagery... But it struck me that for her to modernise and move on she had to take some risks musically and show her more creative side... she was always and is a creatively driven individual.'

Let's Get To It is notable for two things, however: firstly, the cover, with its Juergen Teller shot of Kylie with the hugest lips in history, and secondly it was the first album which features songs written by Kylie. With her departure from SAW, Kylie began further exploring the possibility of writing and its application to her dance/pop productions. Early attempts at songwriting had created simplistic melodies and lyrics, but Kylie was now itching to delve more deeply into her musical potential.

A legacy from her relationship with Michael, Kylie would often scribble down words or lyrics and play with their form and arrangement.

PWL was where I cut my musical teeth and I'm thankful for the lessons I learned there. No one taught me as such but I have an insatiably inquisitive nature and I had lots of time in the studio to absorb things: to watch, listen and learn.

My first steps into the world of songwriting were tentative ones but now I love the creative process and the room that is given for expression and feel very much at home there. The fact that you start a session with nothing and end up with a kind of friend in a new song is so exciting and inspiring. The ultimate reward is having people enjoy and relate to music and songs that I have created.

December 14-21 1994 No.1269 £1.50

Time Out

Complete
8-day
TV
guide

Hits and misses '94

THE CRITS: our best
and worst films, food,
bands, books, products
and performances
THE WITS, shits, gits,
snits and tits of the year
& KYLIE'S KO's and OK's

1-555-CONFIDE

CALL CALL CALL

Steve Anderson and his partner, Dave Seaman, worked under the moniker Brothers in Rhythm. They remixed one of PWL's more graceful moments with the song 'Finer Feelings' and Kylie loved it. Steve was to become one of Kylie's long-term collaborators, and he has been writing many tunes with her over the last seven years.

The Summer of Love in 1988 was the 'official' advent of house music, an eclectic fusion of electronic, disco beats and funk, often using breakbeats. The hitherto exclusive doors of clubland blew open and the underground became mainstream. Suddenly, the technology to create a 'loop' of beats was available and affordable, a four-track mixing desk, decks and samplers were being sold down the high street.

The lack of understanding of any laws governing copyright of covering sampled tracks made it easy to produce home-made dance tracks: DIY disco. It also marked the official birth of the E generation, as legions of teenagers all put on their hooded tops and smiley badges and headed for Ibiza. From that point the boundaries between pop and dance blurred, house music beginning its onslaught of the top ten. Pop became synonymous with dance, but all this also featured a trend towards anonymity: the faceless diva hollering over some dance beat. The charts became overrun with dance one-hit wonders, thus auguring the decline of the pop star as we knew it.

Record bosses swiftly recognised the changes and poured copious amounts of money into 'remixes' wherein you could have a purpose-built pop song of any genre crossing into clubland. DJs and the producers became the pioneers of the dance era and were brought in to increase the sales and maximise potential. With her move to deConstruction, which was a dance label, Kylie began working with names from the dance world, combining a pop sensibility with the innovations of the dance underground.

Brothers in Rhythm were well aware of this crossover and its appeal and realised that Kylie was the perfect vehicle for their own dance/pop hybrids. Her vocal range and willingness to experiment musically meant that Steve and Dave could push the envelope further.

Twelve years later, in a world where DJs are superstars and producers can be as well known as their artists, it is commonplace for artists to be launched in the dance arena. Not then. Kylie's signing to deConstruction was seen by many as a brave move. Whether it actually worked or not depends upon your musical taste, but no one can deny that she was wise to realise the power of dance, and was ahead of her time in constructing a pop album with dance collaborators.

The video for 'Confide In Me' presents Kylie as a kaleidoscope of female stereotypes that at first suggests she is a plastic commodity. This notion is overturned by a lyrical content that reveals, contrarily, a multi-dimensional character who actually empowers.

The message in the lyrics is that it is she who manipulates the situation by saying 'I can keep a secret and throw away the key' and she gains the listeners' respect as the power remains hers. She continues this tease by making any voyeur feel that *they* hold the key to power: 'Stick or twist, the choice is yours'. She offers the choice but still holds the key. She is both key and keyhole, masculine and feminine. This is symbolic of the internal power struggle that rages beneath her surface. She is both puppet and puppet master.

Pete Hadfield commented that deConstruction were expected merely to place Kylie's vocal over a set of house records with a techno edge. His intention was to push things musically as far as he could go. He and Kylie's collaborators on that album were all from the arena of dance: M People, from the deConstruction fold themselves; The Pet Shop Boys; St Etienne and Brothers in Rhythm were all engaged in what Hadfield refers to as 'the re-engineering of Kylie Minogue'. She felt immediately comfortable with her new label: mixes of her songs had been doing the rounds of the DJs for the last few years. PWL had taken a dance genre (Hi-NRG) and made it pop so it was of little surprise that she made the transition back into the clubs with such ease.

There was a tremendous buzz before the release of 'Confide In Me' and deConstruction's marketing division tantalised fans with a series of posters positioned everywhere from bus shelters to tube stations. Pete Hadfield and Co. clearly intended to fulfil their promise to re-engineer the image of Kylie Minogue. The girl on these posters was virtually unrecognisable. Her hair in an Afro of tightly-curled ringlets, a grainy black-and-white Kylie peeked through a Venetian blind. There were no words on the posters, just a date written in simple helvetica type indicating the launch date of the newly regenerated Minogue.

Mark Farrow, award-winning graphic design pioneer, designed the new minimal Kylie packaging and related promotional devices, his slick minimalism and the typeface he favoured symbolising the new ultra 'designed' Kylie. The 'deconstruction' of the record company's name was no irony: Kylie literally *was* deconstructed and modernised as they stripped away the components integral to her pop image.

Hadfield claims, 'We were trying to provoke a reaction in many ways'. Kylie had already become 'cool', but now everything was harmonised in terms of packaging, imagery and music to herald her new credibility. With the first deConstruction album called simply *Kylie Minogue*, they reinvented the diminutive diva as a definitive, credible dance artist.

Kylie's appearance in the first official deConstruction photo shoot is both remarkable and curious. Her ringletted Afro was shot by Ellen Von Unwerth. If you did not know otherwise you could be forgiven for thinking that she was of mixed race origin. The locations and backdrops of graffiti-decorated streets and New York phone booths add to this impression. She is dressed in a style that has become synonymous with Sarah Jessica Parker's character in *Sex and the City*. The racial ambiguities of the photos are indicative of the black origins of many of the leading dance divas and soul singers, automatically providing a visual credence and subtle propaganda that showed that Kylie was now taking herself and her music seriously.

A girlfriend of mine, Charlie Fenn, learnt
how to put hair in rag curls from her
grandmother. We
tried it one night
for fun and it
looked great.
When it came to the
shoot with Ellen, I
suggested we try
it, so Charlie
and I
prepared
it the
night
before
and I
arrived
in the
morning
with a
head full
of rags.

[redacted]

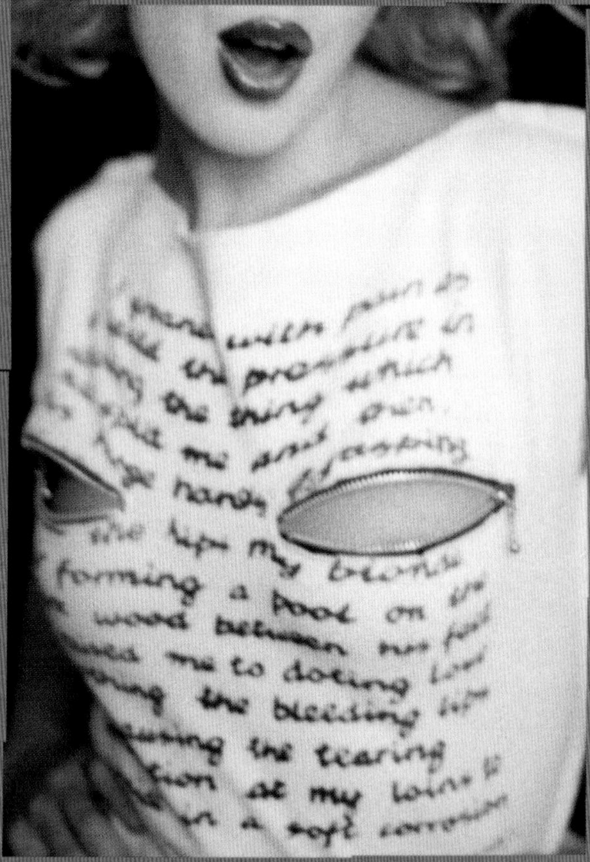

[redacted]

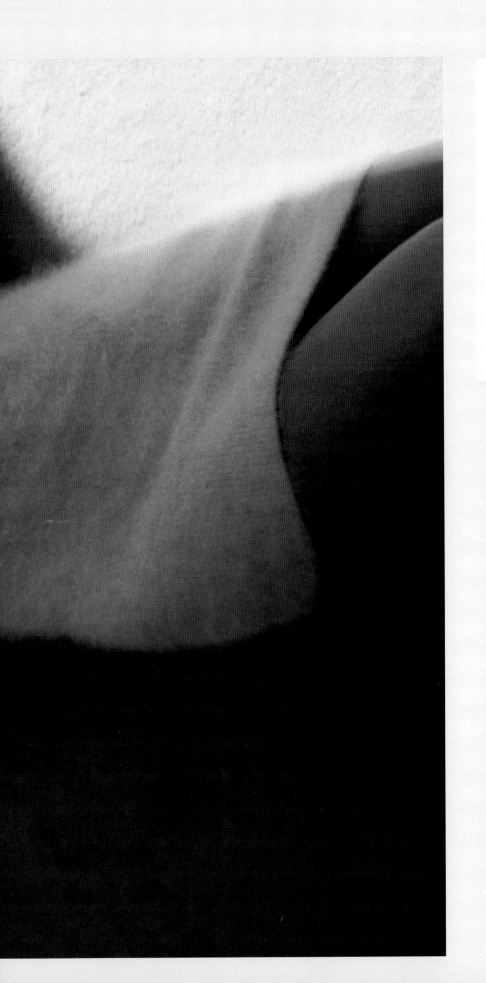

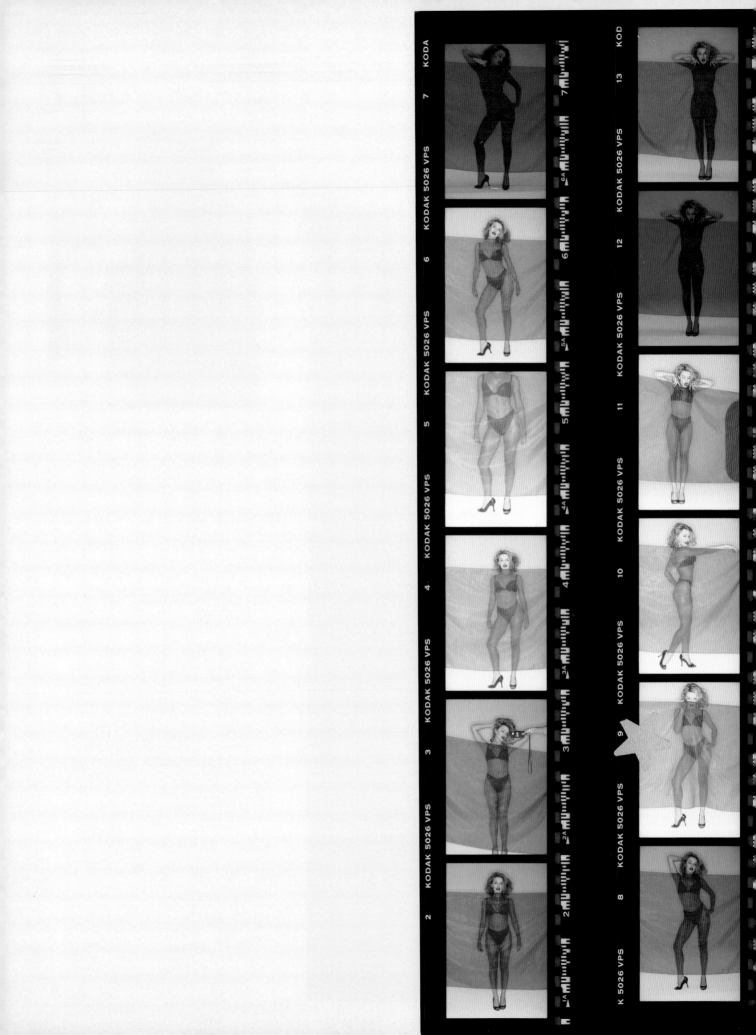

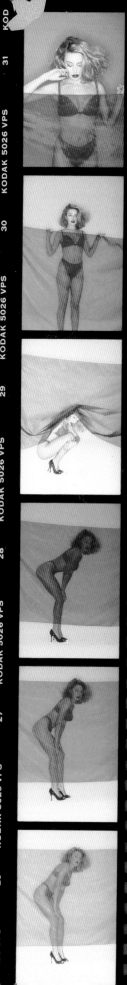

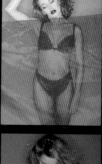

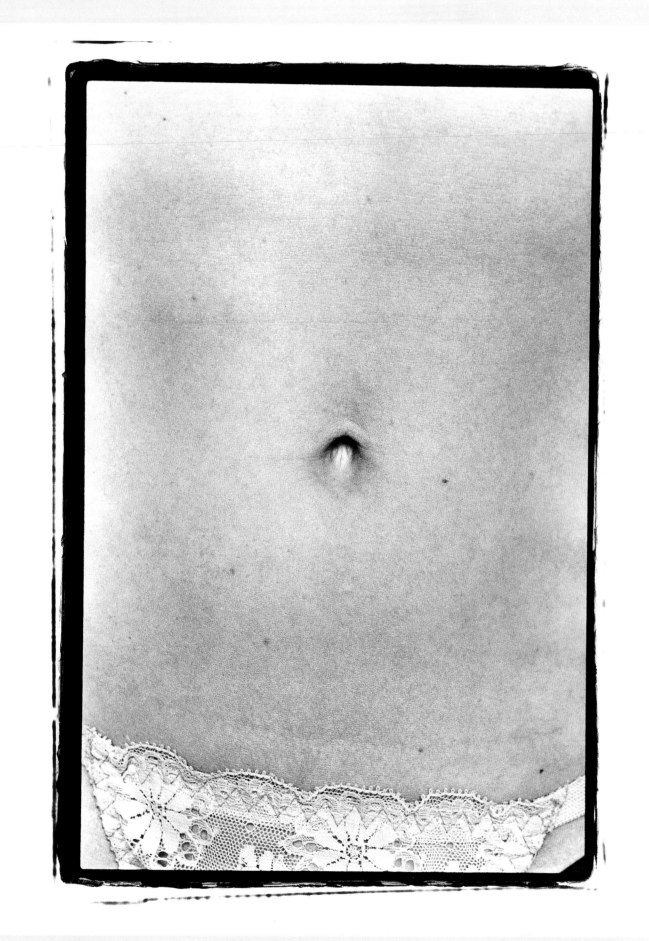

For the album cover deConstruction continued their approach of applying the cutting-edge to Kylie's image. *Dazed & Confused* magazine was then in its infancy, an avant-garde and conceptual publication aiming to fill a gap that the now glossy style bibles *i-D* and *The Face* had missed. Originating as underground publications in the early eighties when style magazines were non-existent, *The Face* and *i-D* were created by and for the notoriously fashionable avant-garde London underground club and art school scene. With the national and subsequent international success of these publications they inevitably became integrated into the mainstream, forsaking the underground as the more commercial demands of advertising revenue assumed greater importance.

Two of *Dazed*'s founders, photographer Rankin and stylist Katie Grand, were pivotal in the developing art/fashion community that flocked to London's East End, where the then cheap rents and deserted industrial spaces made it affordable for young fashion designers, photographers and graphic designers, all fresh out of college, to start up their own businesses in an inspiring and vibrant community – a melting pot of raw, young and very English talent.

The immediate cool of *Dazed* provided the magazine and its contributors with status and ethos. deConstruction wanted to bottle this ethos and apply it to Kylie. As well as photographing and styling the album cover, *Dazed & Confused* published a *Kylie Bible* fanzine featuring her styled in the clothes designed by many of the new wave of English designers.

Rankin and Katie had half a day to shoot the album cover and whatever else they could. A smash room was erected in a parking lot in LA in the blazing sunshine. Roomney's clothing came out of Katie's suitcase, including the suit and glasses used for the cover. There was no hidden meaning behind this outfit, we were just shooting what looked good. We shot enough pictures to sink a ship in Rankin's now infamous speed and ease taking photographs.

Kat and I had our feathers
ruffled by being ousted by these
young cool upstarts. After the
first photo shoot that I hadn't
been allowed to attend, Kat,
Kylie and I had begun spending
more and more time together, with
me styling Kylie and Kat taking
photographs. The first shoot we
all did together was one based
around the idea of the damsel in
distress from old Hollywood
movies. We never managed to tie
Minogue to a train track with her
doom imminently and rapidly
approaching in the background,
but Kat shot her in a variety of
panic-stricken poses, from
swinging across a room on a
chandelier to falling from a
balcony. The shoot took place at
a friend of Kat's country estate
named Romden, and it was the
first time I had spent any length
of time with Kylie, the shoot
taking place over a long weekend.
The stately home's beautiful
location in the typically English
countryside created a relaxed
atmosphere to shoot in, and the
boundaries began to melt away
between us all. That was the
first shoot of many.
   We understood the reasons for
Kylie's re-engineering, but we
felt badly let down, and a short
rift with Kylie ensued. Kylie was
understandably miffed at her two
hotheaded friends, but
commissioned a press shoot with
her old comrades as a peace
offering.

While Kat was setting up shot inside the Katherine Hamnett store on Sloane Street, positioning her lights around a Salvador Dali lip sofa, Kylie, brandishing a coat hanger, cornered me in the changing room. 'I hope you're not turning into a fashion queen,' she declared, eyes raging and coat hanger quivering, dressed in nothing but a flesh-coloured G-string. 'Have you been doggin' me around town?' she continued, coat hanger nearing my throat as she delivered this line as if it had come straight from a Michael Jackson song.

That brief rebuke in the Hamnett changing room struck hard and made me reassess. It is very easy, at the age of twenty-one, to become consumed by the sometimes bitchy, often shallow, but always alluring world of fashion. Everything had really happened so quickly for me and this moment was a turning point for me. I was blinded by my own fabulousness and the lights of cameras flashing, basking in the spotlight intended for my friend. I had been swept away by the London fashion scene. Everything had gone to my head, the dizzying pace of events, the opportunities that had presented themselves as a result of doors opening, and the impact on a naive fresh-faced boy from Manchester of the reality of being friends with a celebrity suddenly crashed home. It was difficult sometimes to distinguish between the girl who was my friend and her pop star alter ego. I'd just been seeing the pop star, the product. I hadn't even thought that this fragile girl had feelings, and she was understandably hurt by the way Kat and I had acted. We were supposed to be her friends, not people whose loyalty depended on us being on her payroll or seeing her as a means to our success.

I would be a fool if I hadn't asked myself what I would have become had I never met Kylie. My future would have been very different. With time came genuine mutual love, affection and respect. But then all I saw was the girl who had been ironing in the Mugler maid's outfit on TV.

To be associated with a pop star has been both a help and a hindrance. If the pop star is riding high one is treated like the star themselves, showered with freebies and invited to all the parties... the moment the star drops out of the top ten the invites, perks and phone-calls stop.

Of course I loved the attention, the fame by association that comes with a famous person/non-famous person friendship. But after a while, the constant questions about my celebrity friend began to grate. Having first bolstered the ego, it can begin to destroy it. All people want to know about is Kylie. At times I have felt that I have ceased to be myself and instead have just become Kylie's handbag. Of course socially it was inevitable that Kylie became a carrot to dangle, a luring into a fragile delicate world that in reality is a house of cards. I discovered it is dangerous to use someone else to uphold your own self-esteem. I learned quickly, but it was a hard lesson.

The second single from *Kylie Minogue* was 'Put Yourself In My Place'. The cover was another Rankin shot, this time of Kylie wearing headphones, another symbol of her new 'serious' approach depicting her clearly listening to music. It was all too much for Virgin Radio which embarked on a poster campaign declaring that they had done the one thing to improve Kylie's records and banned them, as if she was an ambassador for and symbolic of all bad music – another example of people having no appreciation that behind those records, underneath the celebrity is a human being.

At first sight, the posters were indeed funny, but for the person under attack and being used to bolster the other's credibility, it was another painful cross to bear. Years later Kylie slapped the faces of the executives concerned live on Chris Evans' breakfast show on Virgin Radio, her very presence there already a revenge of sorts.

On live radio I had four execs who literally had no choice but to take it on the chin. I just thought they should know it wasn't nice. Standing in front of them is the best way to make it understood that there are emotions involved. It was worse for the second, third and fourth guy as they had witnessed the velocity and accuracy of my slap to the face of the first person and knew what was coming. The atmosphere in the studio was fantastic. I savoured my cold dish of revenge, Chris Evans, the host, was in fits of laughter, and though the poor executives had to endure some pain and humiliation, I'm sure they have dined out on the story more than once.

The video for 'Put Yourself In My Place' remains one of Kylie's favourites.

It was one of my more painful shoots (they all seem to hurt in one way or another). I was rigged into all sorts of contraptions - hanging from the ceiling in a harness, balancing on the 'butt plate' and 'stomach plate' - and shimmied onto a dolly with a revolving disc on the end. Trusty fohney wire made my clothing float off into space. It was big hair, big lashes and a pink space suit and after two nineteen hour days I had had enough of all these things. Video days are like a time-warp. You lose all touch with the outside world and reality but I absolutely love making them. I've ended up in tears numerous times.

NO MORE VIDEOS IN WATER OR HARNESSES !!

A sumptuous striptease in space, based upon Jane Fonda's Barbarella, the video was the first in which Kylie removed her clothes and one of the earliest videos to explore human flight. This slice of space fantasy was a precursor of her more explicit striptease in 2001 - in the notorious cinema commercial for lingerie conceptualists Agent Provocateur. In 'Put Yourself In My Place' there are touches of Fonda about her long blonde hair, full lips and great dark eyes. Again she plays with image stereotype, the enchanting space warrior alone amongst the stars in her spacecraft. As the saucy dominatrix in the Agent ad, she again entices her viewers, daring them to watch her writhe on a red velvet bucking bronco. Her stiletto heels are a gleaming black, feet perfectly arched. Her underwear is sheer and also black, revealing, but not too much, decorative rather than vulgar display. All the traditional garb of erotica was present in the commercial: stockings, suspenders, heels, bra and knickers, the lines of the garments accentuating every curve.

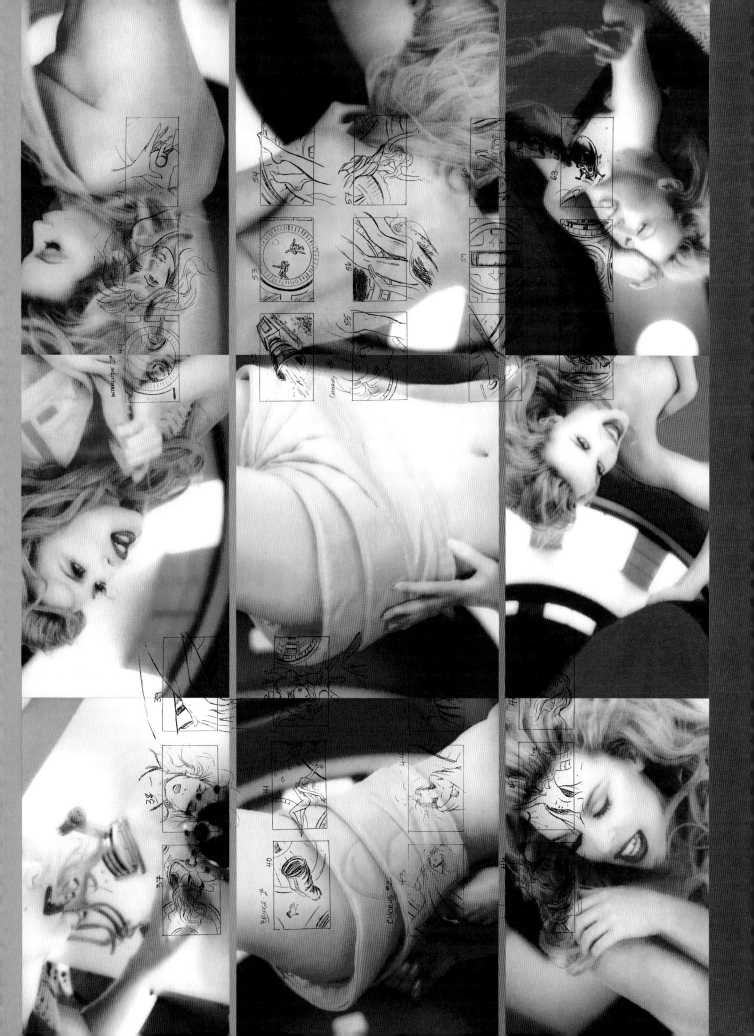

Both advert and video begin
with Kylie fully clothed, an
essential ingredient offering a
form of audience participation in
the tease. As Richard Wortley,
author of *A Pictorial History of
the Striptease*, remarked:

'In essence, the striptease is an
act in which dancer and audience
connive: it begins with the
dancer wearing clothes and
follows a predictable, and to
some extent comforting, routine
until the dancer is naked,
available to be admired, but not
to be interfered with (except in
the mind).'

The colours of her spacesuit and
Agent Provocateur uniform include
differing shades of pink, a
colour, along with red and
purple, so often symbolising
aroused passion. In 'Put Yourself
In My Place', the tones are
bleached and hi-contrast, the
primary colours and pinks
pulsating from the screen
reflecting increased arousal. The
shades of the Agent ad are much
more natural: golden skin, pastel
pinks, deep reds and black, but
again all shades which have
sexual significance.

   Vincent Peters, photographer,
observed of Kylie:

'I think she owns that cute sexy
space. She knows very well how to
define the line between being
cheeky and sexy, but she is never
vulgar, it's always a bit of a
game, and I think whatever she
does, you never know if she
really means it.'

Agent Provocateur co-owner Serena Rees adds:

'She enjoys who she is as a woman, she celebrates her femininity, she's proud of herself, still strong and powerful but not in a threatening way. She's sexy, flirtatious... you want to spend time with her.'

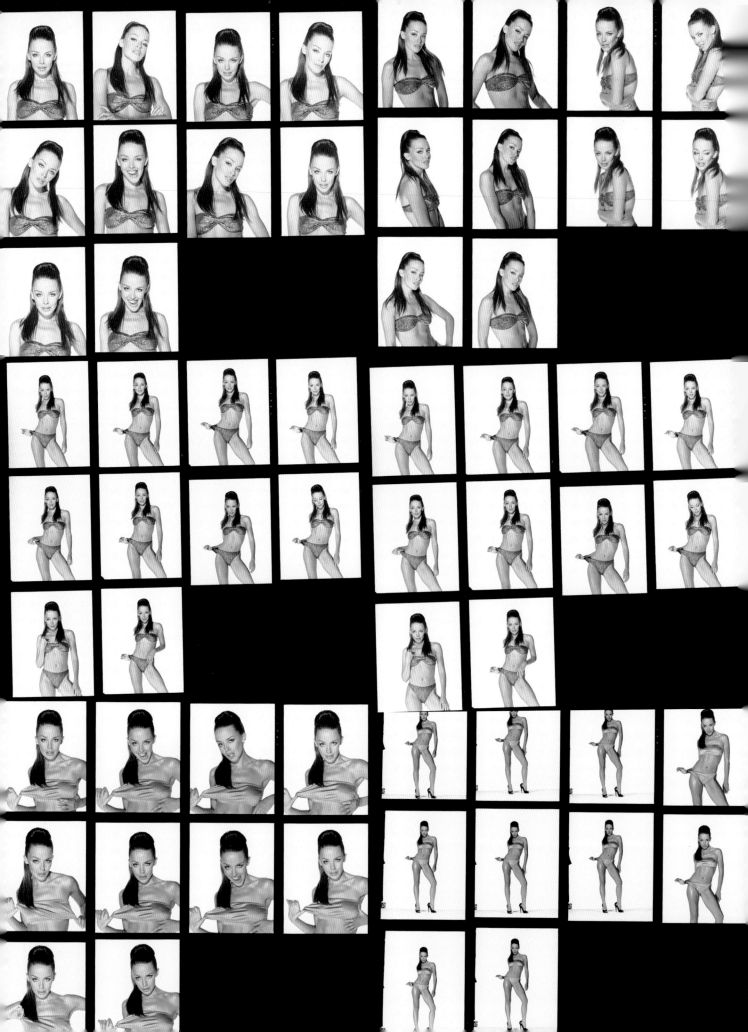

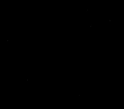

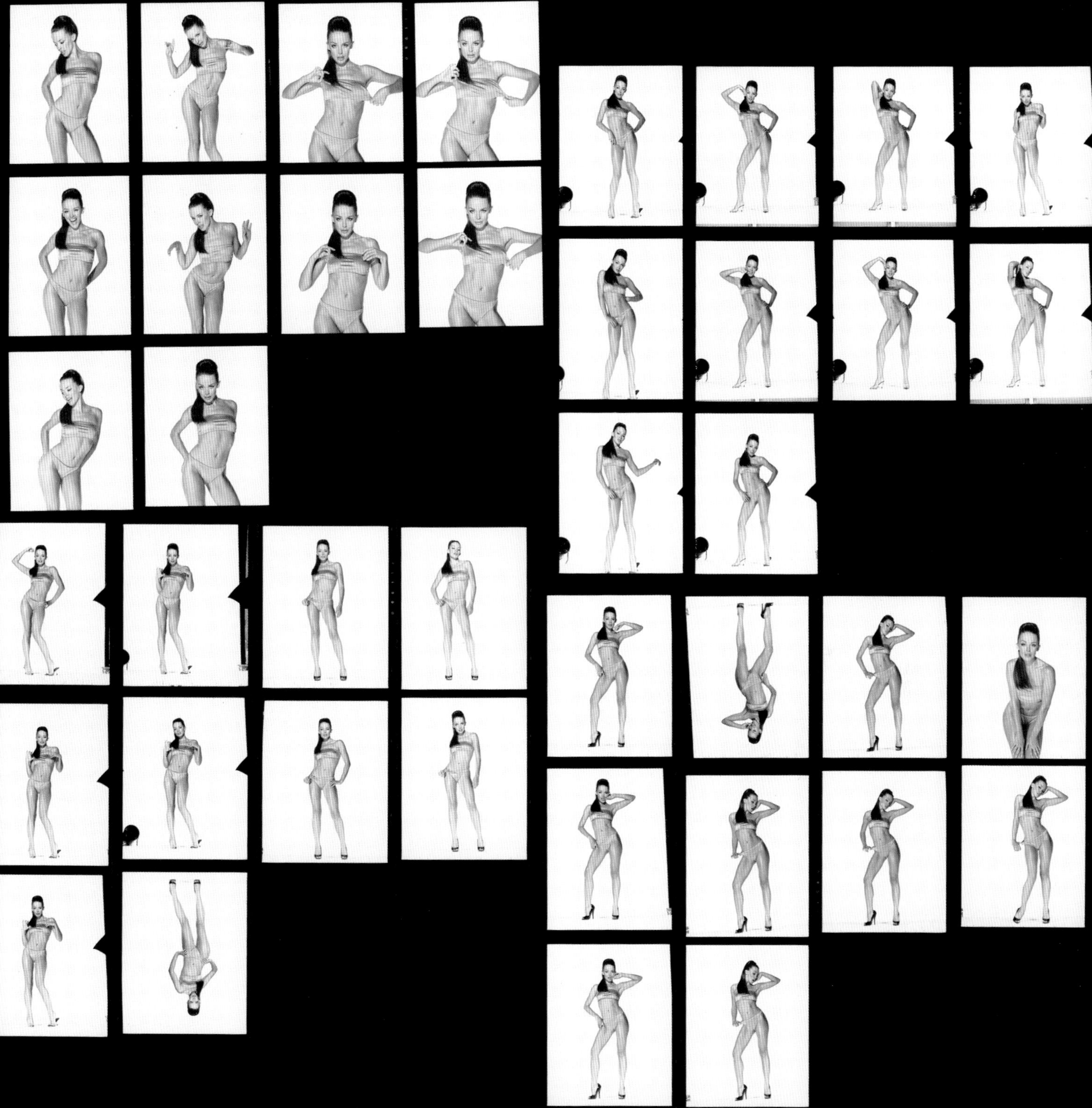

Brrr- Cold (once again) on
video for 'Where Is the Feeling.

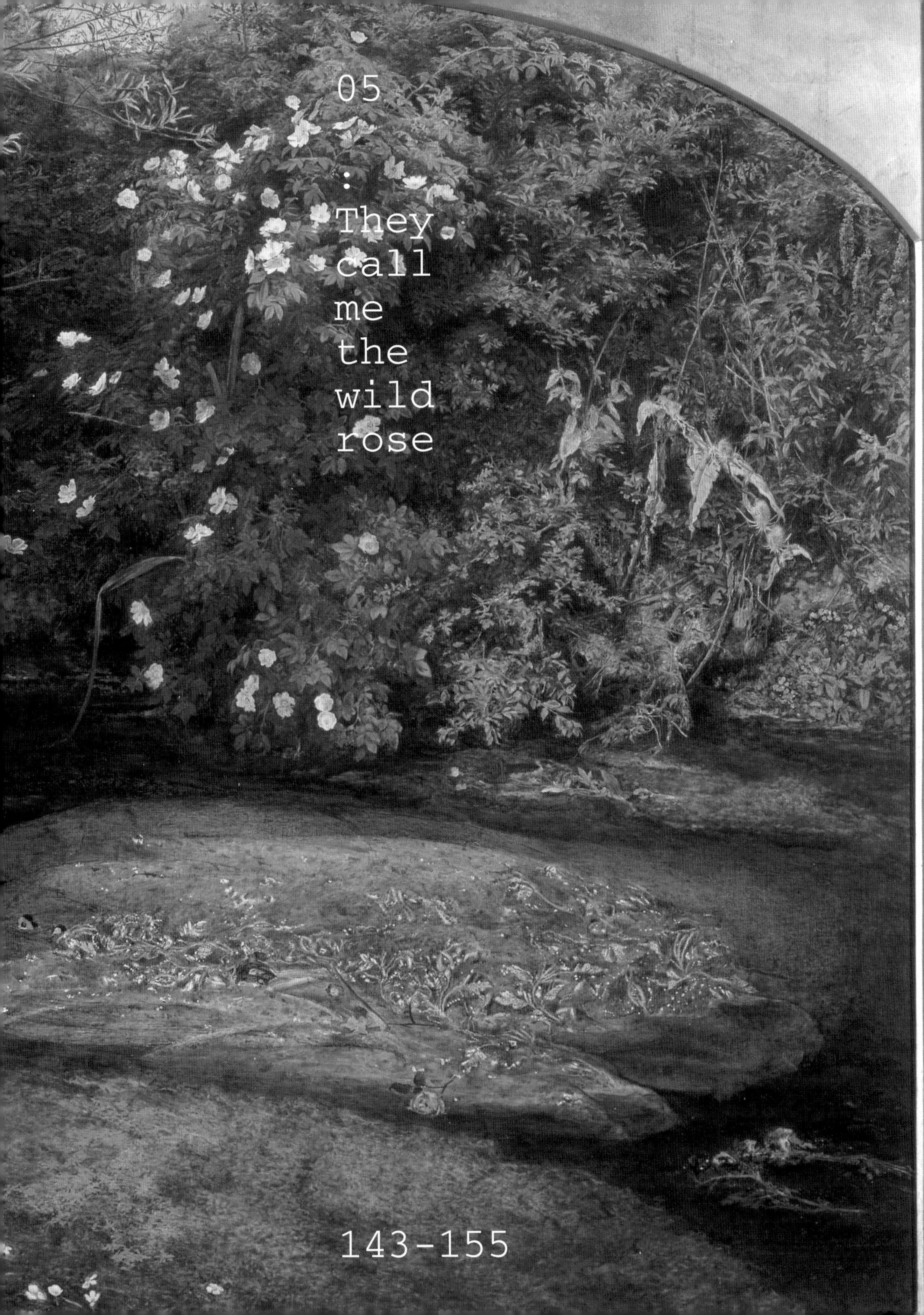

05 : They call me the wild rose

143-155

Collaborations pave the way for an interesting experience.
I'm always intrigued by what I don't know.

7 October 1995   80p $(US)3.95

DAMON GUN DRAMA – Page 3

NME

NEW MUSICAL EXPRESS

Life and loves of a sheila-devil

Germany Dm 5.30 Spain Psa 330

Wonderwail: NOEL GALLAGHER mouths off (again)

SUPERGROUPS:
latest league results

KD LANG ★ GREEN DAY
THE BLUETONES ★ PULP
JOSH WINK ★ SLEEPER
NORTHERN UPROAR
THE BOO RADLEYS
EDDIE IZZARD
JULIAN COPE
SIMPLY RED
MENSWEAR

DYING FOR IT!
NICK and KYLIE's dangerous liaison

9 770028 636055

I remember it was years before that Michael had told me about his friend Nick who wanted to work with me. I had heard of him but was unaware of the legend of Nick Cave. At that time, 'The Birthday Party' and 'The Bad Seeds' were not in my collection. I didn't attempt to find out more about it, not sure if it was just a passing comment.

A few years later I saw some reportages tour shots of Nick and The Bad Seeds. Nick had a vinyl shoulder bag with 'KYLIE' emblazoned on it. It was still some time after that that I received a phone call from Mushroom Records saying They had a demo for a duet with Nick Cave and could They send it over. Instinctively I knew that this curious and unlikely collaboration, in the form of a murder ballad no less, would work. I just could never have guessed how well.

'Where The Wild Roses Grow' was a love song from a murderous lover to a victim whose haunting beauty had so entranced him that he sought to preserve her perfection in the tranquil repose of death. Kylie's video character, Elisa Day, almost colluded in her impending demise. The mood of the video was ethereal and erotic, the director apparently inspired by TV's infamously unsubtle Flake ads, and there was a tense underlying admission of the tug of necrophilia: the murderer broods upon his victim, dead in a lake, whilst the pale, flame-haired and crimson-lipped ghost of Kylie drifts amongst meadows of blood-red flowers, a symbolic python slithering across the former pop princess's nether regions as her corpse lies half-submerged in the reed-fringed water.

The image of Kylie floating dead in the lake is a fairly literal interpretation of Millais' painting of *Hamlet*'s drowned Ophelia. The python representing temptation and the scarlet roses true love echo the several symbolic elements in Millais' painting. In the book *I'm A Man* by Ruth Padel, Cave said simply:

'I've always enjoyed writing songs about dead women.'

Curiously, Kylie's flatmate Kat had also photographed her apparently dead in a bath years earlier as if the silence and peace of what Shakespeare called 'the undiscovered country' was somehow an appropriate environment for Kylie's Lolita-like, child-woman beauty. Kat's interpretation employs a red approximation of the fragile lace dress that Millais' Ophelia wore as the half-submerged Kylie lies still, apparently drowned. In folklore a red dress symbolised the passage from girlhood into womanhood. Here it symbolised a darker passage.

The song gave Cave the highest chart position of his career and even Kylie's fiercest critics grudgingly agreed that the 'Singing Budgie' had been silenced in this intense evocation of music's more cerebral prowess and the serious themes and subtexts which the macabre video addressed. It proved that the girl who used to blow bubble bath into the camera had definitely become a woman, one whose natural beauty had matured into timeless and erotic femininity. Cave's vision enabled all Kylie's fragile delicacy and her deepest complexities to be revealed at last.

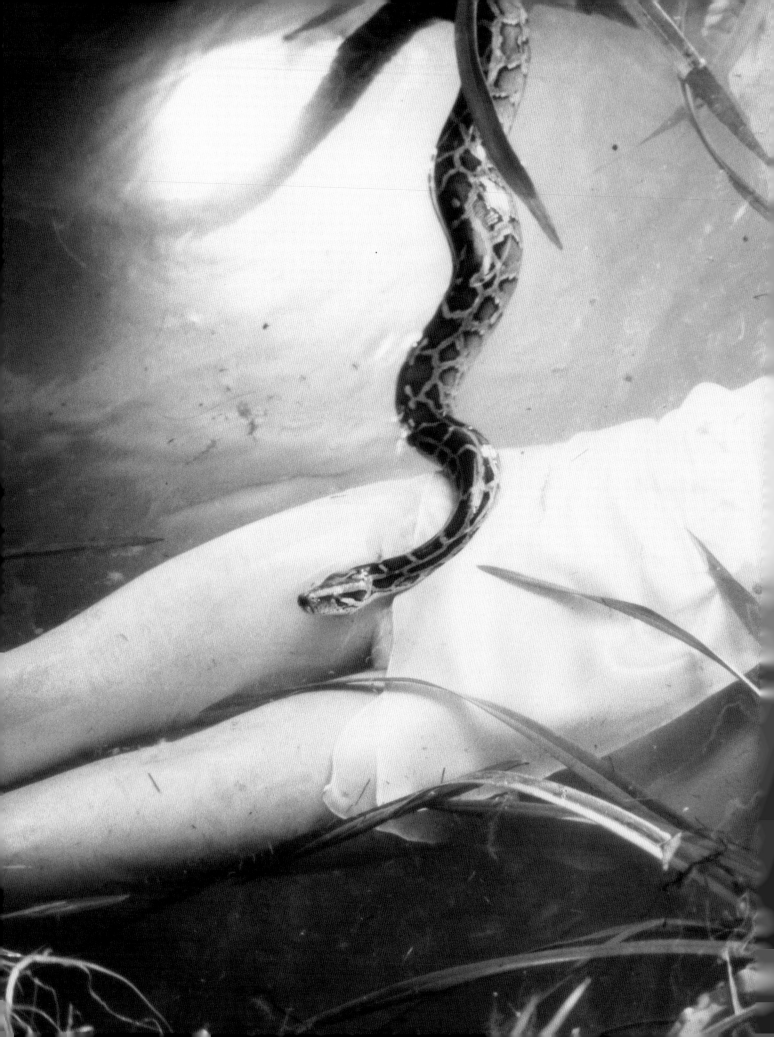

I first met Nick on the day I recorded my vocals. Prior to that our attempts at communication had been limited to phone-tag messages between our respective mothers, which was quite funny. My performance on the record was something of a revelation to me. I had never sounded like that before. Nick was ever so lovely and very gentle, directing me to achieve that sound, to bring alive the characters and the story. We only did a few takes and it was very natural and easy. I think that the fact that it was our first encounter enhanced the performance and it made way for the gentle, exciting and dangerous sexual tension within the story. It meant so much to me that he hadn't just come up with a quick idea to do a post-modern duet; he had thought about it for years and waited and waited until the time and the song were right. [...] a man and a talent; he has inspired me greatly. In fact there is nothing that I have done with him in various shows and performances that hasn't been meaningful and tremendously rewarding.

Some live versions of the song
itself were equally, if
differently, memorable. Kylie
often guested with Cave at his
concerts both here and in
Australia. She enjoyed this,
relieved to have none of the
pressures and responsibilities of
promoting and carrying her own
shows. For a performance on *Top
of the Pops* she wore a
distressed, tattered lace dress
from Alexander McQueen's Highland
Rape collection, with pale make-
up and flowers in her hair. For
another performance, she wore a
green dress by Owen Gaster, a
quiet skateboarder from Sussex,
with devoré beetles crawling all
over it. It fitted the Goth opera
fantasy surrounding her dead
alter ego.

Cave asked Kylie back to
feature the song in his 2000
Meltdown Festival but this time
to 'enact' it with another famous
Australian export, Sir Les
Patterson, filthy compatriot of
Dame Edna Everage, both created
and played by Barry Humphries.
Kylie was as enchanting as ever
as she once again donned the damp
lace of Elisa Day and seduced her
vulgar vanquisher with wit as
well as beauty. As she lay dead
at Sir Les's feet she murmured,
'And he knelt above me with a
rock in his fist'. Salivating Sir
Les seized the moment and
unleashed a twelve-inch
prosthetic piece from the depths
of his stained Y-fronts and
brandished it behind her head.

It was so funny. I was thrilled to be working with the great
Barry Humphries. We had rehearsed the song and we had
both agreed to perform it straight - it would be funnier that way.
Well, there's no accounting for performers in front of an audience
and Sir Les got a bit excited. When his antics began, I was so
shocked I couldn't bring myself to look and ran to the other
side of the stage. I think Sir Les impressed the Royal Albert Hall.

06

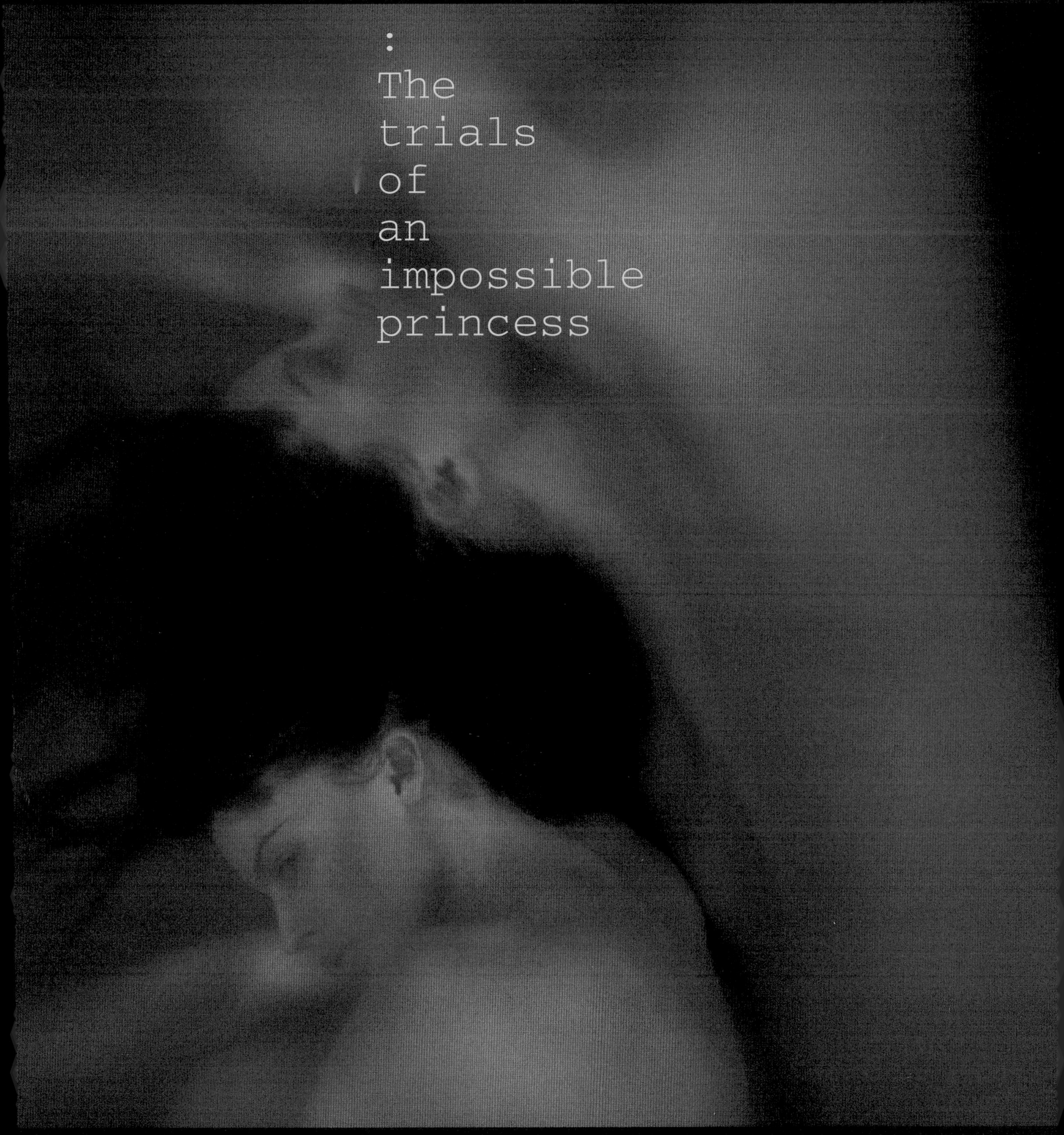

:
The trials of an impossible princess

157–187

Impossible Princess, Kylie's second deConstruction album, at almost two years in the making, was the longest Kylie had worked on anything since her soapsud days of *Neighbours*. It was no coincidence that these drawn-out years in 1997 and 1998 coincided with an intense romance with French video director and photographer Stephane Sednaoui. He was a creative powerhouse, six feet tall with a shaved head embellished with two little styled horns and a rat's tail at the back. He usually wore Japanese army trousers, Nike airs and fleece jackets that looked like they hadn't been washed for years. He looked liked a cosmic hobo.

Rooted in Paris, New York, LA and nowhere in particular, his videos for Björk, Red Hot Chili Peppers, Alanis Morissette and Fiona Apple, among others, were odes to the simple luxury of freedom. The video for Morissette's 'Ironic' was set on a long freeway drive with no end and no conceivable beginning, and the Björk video featured her on the back of a truck in downtown Manhattan, simply performing in the open air of the city.

Since they had met at a party in London's East End to celebrate ten years of *The Face* magazine, this Sometime Samurai had turned twenty-eight-year-old Kylie's life upside down. In her songs she often described him using the metaphors of Eastern mysticism. 'From the temple, won't you stay a while...' Her description of him as an urban Buddhist punk somehow explains his influence on her, hinting at a relationship of guru/teacher and disciple. The song 'Sometime Samurai', the result of a collaboration with Towa Tei and Kylie, has never been released but included the lines 'Man of the moment, possibly all time, sing to me a lullaby...' 'Cowboy Style' echoed and expanded her sentiments: 'Shed my skin when you came in, Where do you end and I begin...', capturing the metamorphosis that Kylie was to undergo during the relationship.

'Impossible Princess' isn't about being a prima donna. At the time I was being quite impossible, not for other people, but for myself. The title refers to the complexities and contradictions within me. I was fascinated by the way words sounded and was being impossible in my belief in possibility.

Rarely had Kylie felt so alive. She embarked on a series of adventures that in hindsight seemed more like quests of self-discovery, from a month on the road in Sednaoui's vintage trans-am, accompanied only by a large stuffed Pink Panther, from New York to LA, to escapes to the glacial slopes of Whistler where Kylie took up snowboarding with her usual irritating ease. Then to the markets of downtown Tokyo and Southern China where, armed with her new toy, a Contax camera, she joyfully photographed anything that interested her.

Away from the pressure of paparazzi, her sense of freedom intensified as Stephane instilled and nurtured in her a deep sense of her own creativity and talent. This release and adventurousness were captured in another song intended for *Impossible Princess* and written during their road trip. 'This is the feeling, I want for always... free.' In the arms of Stephane, Kylie shed the skin of the two-dimensional pop princess she had thought she had escaped by signing to deConstruction. It wasn't that she wanted to be taken seriously by others, more that she realised that she was worthy of taking herself and all her many contradictions more seriously.

Sednaoui had introduced her to several musicians. The work of Shirley Manson and Garbage, Björk, Tricky, Mirwais and U2 inspired her, and along with her collaboration with Nick Cave opened up whole new possibilities for a new personal direction. Kylie had never before dared to think that anyone was remotely interested in what she felt and who she was. She developed admiration for self-expressive modern artists Tracey Emin and Sam Taylor-Wood, who asked her to star in her short film, *Misfit*, which featured a naked Kylie miming to *The Last Castrato*. Misfit was indeed an apt description of Kylie at the time.

She fervently devoured new music, particularly enjoying the peculiar blends of Japanese and French pop favoured by G Love and Special Sauce, Towa Tei, Pizzicato Five and more obscure underground dance artists. She became interested in photography, particularly that of Japanese artist Nobuyoshi Araki, whose colourful images of Japanese women managed to maintain a sense of dangerously seductive and powerful femininity, also present in his sumptuously sexual studies of flowers.

Araki's inspiration is evident in many of the photographs Stephane took of Kylie during this period, many of them featuring Minogue styled in kimonos and culminating in the only video Stephane made for Kylie, 'German Bold Italic', another collaboration with Towa Tei. It portrays her as a demented cyber geisha running around the streets and subways of New York.

Kylie and I spent days traipsing around the costume houses of New York looking for the perfect authentic kimono and obe, eventually finding them in a tiny Greenwich Village emporium, which also kindly supplied a lady to put the complicated ensemble on. It was completed with gorgeous lacquered green Japanese platforms that Stephane had given to Kylie after one of his trips to Japan, and with a pink rubber whip, which later made a guest appearance in former Spice Girl Geri Halliwell's video for 'Bag It Up' and which was purchased from a shop notable for its extensive range of penis enlargers that had caught our eye. Kylie's slap, delicately and laboriously applied by the fabulously outrageous Hollywood make-up artiste supreme, Paul Starr, was a combination of traditional geisha and New Romantic. Lastly came an extraordinarily heavy platinum wig, crammed with as many Japanese cocktail sticks as the piece would allow. Kylie's video

performance was deliberately jerky and manic as she tried to balance the wig equivalent of the Taj Mahal on her self-described pinhead, without toppling over. The shoot was on a freezing New York winter day and Stephane filmed her with a hand-held digicam, running all over the city with the biting Atlantic wind whistling around her bare legs. The sight of this bizarre creature running amok in the streets and subways elicited no comment, nonchalance being a typical response of the residents of the Big Apple.

Stephane loved Japan and the imagery associated with it. Its poppier than pop disposable culture, with its undercurrents of ancient traditions, particularly those associated with the geisha mystique, also appealed to Kylie. The novel *Memoirs of a Geisha* transported her into that exotic world. The idea of the geishas as decorated entertainers of men, their routines and rituals of adorning their bodies and decorating their faces and concealing their true nature behind an impenetrable white mask, struck a definite chord.

Sednaoui saw Kylie as a combination of geisha and manga superheroine, two extreme Japanese interpretations of femininity: powerful, dynamic, seductive and entrancing, yet somehow masked and tied to the invisible bonds of her own tradition - her pop celebrity life.

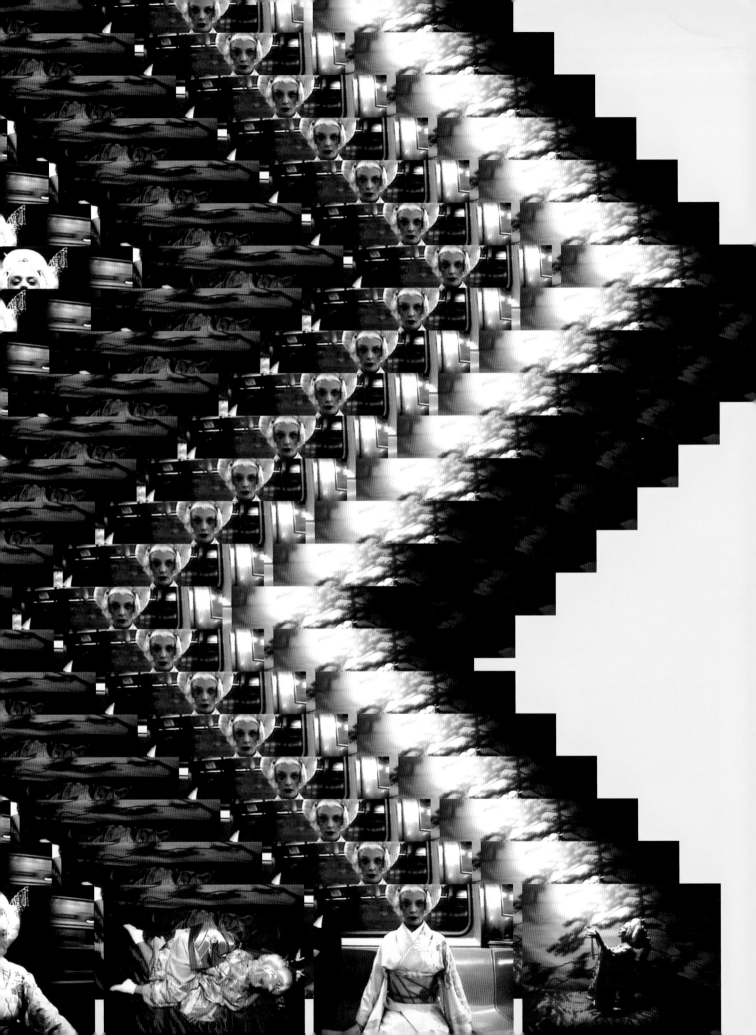

The manga babe was intended to be a theme for the *Impossible Princess* photo shoot and London rubber/fetish designer Stephen Fuller created two rubber catsuits for it, one pale pink and silver, the other metallic blue with side panels cut out. The man from The Little Shoe Box in north London created two pairs of the highest patent stillies you've ever seen but the *pièce de résistance* was still to come.

My assistant and close friend Neil Rodgers, aka Jackie to my Joan, found the most fantastic pair of silicon tits, bearing a remarkable resemblance to chicken fillets, complete with stick-on nipples for that extra realistic touch. These were intended to help create the exaggerated fantasy silhouette of the Japanese animated characters. They provided us with hours of delight as we preened around Neil's flat, proud of our 34 double-D chests, polaroiding our new assets. I was delighted years later when Kylie found the chicken fillets at the bottom of a drawer and sent them home to me by courier. Alas, the shoot never happened.

Kylie discarded the trinkets and paraphernalia of her pop persona, chucking out bags of clothes to the op shop. She ditched the make-up and defiantly cropped her hair with the zeal of someone joining a new order. Her wardrobe became filled with the avant-garde designs of Junya Wattanabe, whose garments played with distortion of the female form, and young British designers, who in their own way were pushing back the frontiers of pattern-cutting.

Owen Gaster designed many garments for her, including gorgeous devoré dresses featuring insects and similar motifs, and complex geometric-based tailoring. Wattanabe had taken his lines outwards and away from the body and Gaster took his inwards, encasing the female form in a series of intricate, angled points. Veronique Leroy, a petite

Belgian designer who was actually the same size as Kylie, created a collection that was all fluoro-coloured lycra, copious amounts of black PVC and netting. It was one of Veronique's dresses that Stephane bought for Kylie that was chosen for her to wear on the cover of *Impossible Princess*.

Stephane, though supportive, was heavily critical of his protégée so Kylie began work on her voice. Instead of just stepping into the recording booth without prior preparation, the One Take Wonder took singing lessons, keen to expand her range and experiment with different delivery styles. She was constantly writing, scribbling words and sentences, playing with their form and meaning, and her new engagement with her inner depths proved relatively easy after years as a devout follower of the ostrich philosophy of life – that of burying the head in the sand and hoping it will all go away.

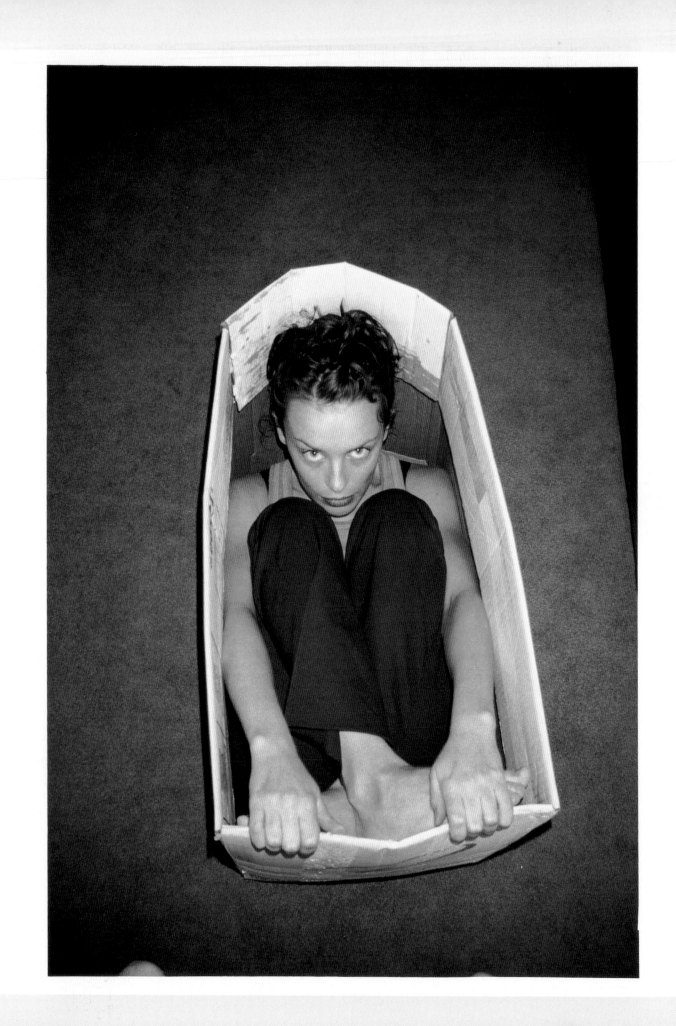

Emotions were gushing like blood from a freshly-open wound. Years of bondage to the pop machine and of inner turmoil had apparently taken their toll and the resulting words seethed with brooding contradictions about lost and suppressed identity and claustrophobic panic, littered with metaphors of chaos, anger and servitude. She describes her mind as a 'snare', of being lost in crossfire, of constant limbo, and there are continual references to her burning 'senses'.

As she emptied her mind into her ever-present notebook, the pain and confused embarrassment of her past gradually began to subside. As far as she was concerned her SAW years were taboo, a closed book that she would have burned had she had the chance. Confronted by the fanzines and annuals from those years which I unearthed at charity shops just to wind her up, she would laugh lightly but secretly rage at the girl staring out at her.

At the Poetry Olympics at London's Albert Hall, while I chatted Damon Albarn up on the dressing-room sofa, masquerading as a Chelsea supporter and drinking flirtatiously from my plastic cup, Nick Cave persuaded Kylie to recite the lyrics of 'I Should Be So Lucky' at the end of his set. Kylie, panic-stricken at the thought, unprepared and dressed in green track pants, an old purple top, no make-up, no bra and with an 'access all areas' pass stuck to her right breast, disrupted my seduction, her horror heightened by the fact that she had forgotten the words.

Somehow the catchy mantra had become deeply etched on my consciousness and I managed to scribble down one verse and chorus, which she delivered in dead-pan manner with all the ironic discomfort of an ashamed schoolgirl being bollocked in morning assembly. The audience seemed uneasy at first and then warmed to her performance as they cottoned on to what she was reciting, laughing with her and not at her. This was a turning point, a milestone, as she later said.

Reading Festival →

Before the 'Poetry Olympics'

It was like being face to face with the girl from my past. Possibly the most cathartic moment I can remember. It felt as if that moment could not have happened a minute earlier or later. At at once I realised you can run but you can't hide and the best thing I could do was to accept the past, to embrace it, to use it. For years I had felt embarrassed and trapped by the person that I was perceived to be. I think people are blinded by my early success and forget the often painful criticism I had to endure. With this realisation and from that moment onwards, everything became so much easier. It was beyond just being postmodern, it was a revelation and a necessity.

She continued to embrace her past with her usual sense of style, humour and irony in Pedro Romanyi's video for 'Did It Again' which featured four Kylies, each defined by the labels that the media had created for her, in a line-up for crimes unmentioned, against a *Usual Suspects*-style criminal backdrop. A one-woman 'trailer' of The Spice Girls, Kylie was split into the various splinters of her pop star persona. Dance Kylie, Cute Kylie, Sex Kylie and Indie Kylie all struggled for supremacy as they battled bitchily with each other for attention.

We made all the costumes ourselves. Sex Kylie was pure drag queen, her get-up made from a cheap piece of vile snake-printed turquoise lycra accessorised with hooker's slingbacks and a Bet Lynch-style leopard coat that had previously featured in 'What Do I Have To Do?'. Sex Kylie was a snarling bitch of a creature, with her split ends, copious amounts of black eyeliner and the slut shoes from Kylie's own Imelda Marcos-sized collection. Dance Kylie, with her irritating frothiness, permanent grin, forever shimmying hips and bubblegum perm was dressed in strips of multicoloured lycra based on a top designed by Stella McCartney that we had used for a shoot for Australian *Vogue*. She wore Kylie's favourite show pony shoes, gold-heeled numbers with diamanté-studded straps that she swore brought her luck on stage. Cute Kylie was suitably nauseating in violet-tasselled hot pants and bra top that we were forced to knock up on the morning of the shoot, the original outfit being in danger of disappearing into the blue screen background on which we were shooting. Indie Kylie was cool and nonchalant in burgundy pedal pushers and *Star Trek*-style top by a designer called Amric, who sold in the much-missed South Molton Street emporium of young British fashion, Pellicano. This outfit was completed with another pair of favourite Manolos, red suede four-inchers, with tassels trailing from the arch of each foot. The video was hilarious, Kylie hamming it up as the different caricatures kicked the shit out of each other.

Her musical collaborators on *Impossible Princess*, a title Kylie devised as an apt description of how she saw her dissatisfied self, were varied. Stalwart companion and producer Steve Anderson and Brothers in Rhythm, the Grid and Towa Tei created slick slices of electronic dance to accompany her tortured lyrics, but A&R man Pete Hadfield was disturbed by the bleakness and hardcore dance styles of 'Too Far' and 'Limbo' in particular – two of my favourite songs for those very reasons.

In fact deConstruction's A&R department, who had so meticulously crafted her previous record, hadn't really been present for much of the album's development due to Pete Hadfield's poor health, so creative control of the project was left with Kylie and Stephane. Such was the power of released emotions from Minogue, surging forward after years of suppression, that the resulting songs were stylistically all over the place and deConstruction were worried that there was no obvious single.

Enter the Manic Street Preachers. The Manics swiftly created two melodious guitar-based numbers for Kylie, 'Some Kind Of Bliss' and 'I Don't Need Anyone', which satisfied deConstruction, but they stuck out from the dance tracks on the rest of the album. Pete Hadfield later added that he thought that *Impossible Princess* was two albums sandwiched together.

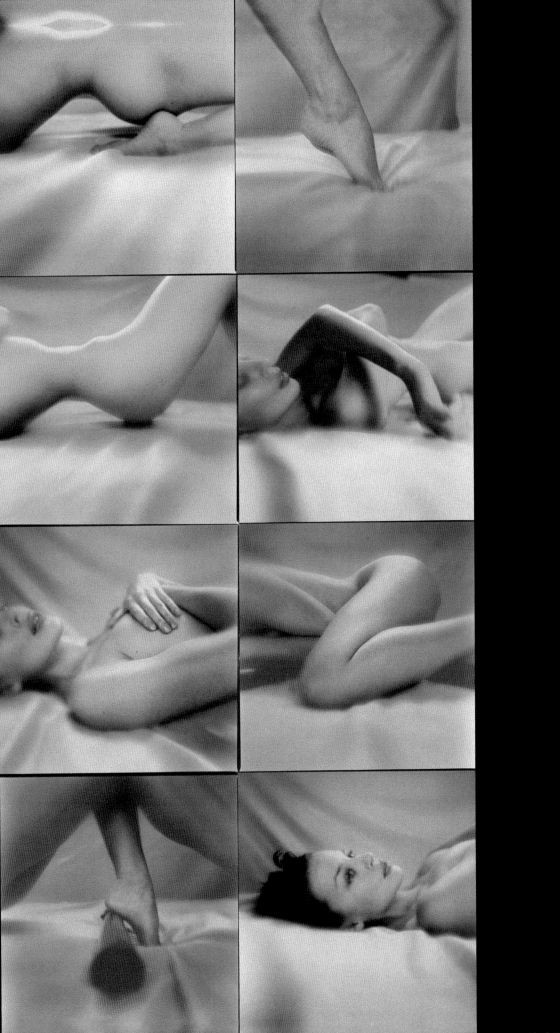

With Kylie and Stephane nearing
the end of their relationship,
the photo shoots for the album
cover were not the easiest of
times. After months of work
deConstruction suddenly announced
the release date and flung
everybody, especially Stephane,
into a panic. Stephane and Kylie
wanted to produce a special
package for the CD with a three-
dimensional cover to represent
the more three-dimensional person
she had become.

Everything seemed to be going
wrong around that time. Even my
prep trip to Paris to gather
clothes for the photo shoot was
disastrous, with me and my
assistant Neil almost coming to
blows on the Eurostar over a pair
of Helmut Lang Y-fronts that I'd
nicked from a PR.
Jealous of the
actually rather dowdy
khaki
underpants,
he
'accidentally' chucked a
cup of boiling coffee all over my
leg as I was on the phone to my
then idiot boyfriend who, I found
out, had mislaid my keys in a
drunken stupor the night before
and was subsequently locked out
of my flat. Thus, armed with
bags of priceless
couture
borrowed from
the fashion houses
of glamorous Paris,
we sat in the pissing
rain outside my Charing
Cross Road flat as the
brown paper bags gradually
disintegrated in the downpour,
chasing after tramps who rather
fancied themselves in the Thierry
Mugler corsets and Veronique
Leroy dresses we were guarding as
we waited for a locksmith.

Tensions were high on the
shoot. It dragged on for a week
and we often didn't leave the
studio until two or three in the
morning. Shooting in 3-D required
a number of static cameras and a
model capable of retaining a
pose, still as marble, for what
seemed like an eternity. Stephane
set up the cameras and then
called for a backdrop of
swirling, coloured lights
achieved by him dressing up like
a cat burglar in black balaclava
and full blackout gear whilst
running around his subject like a
possessed Samurai with a kitchen
light covered with coloured
plastic gels.

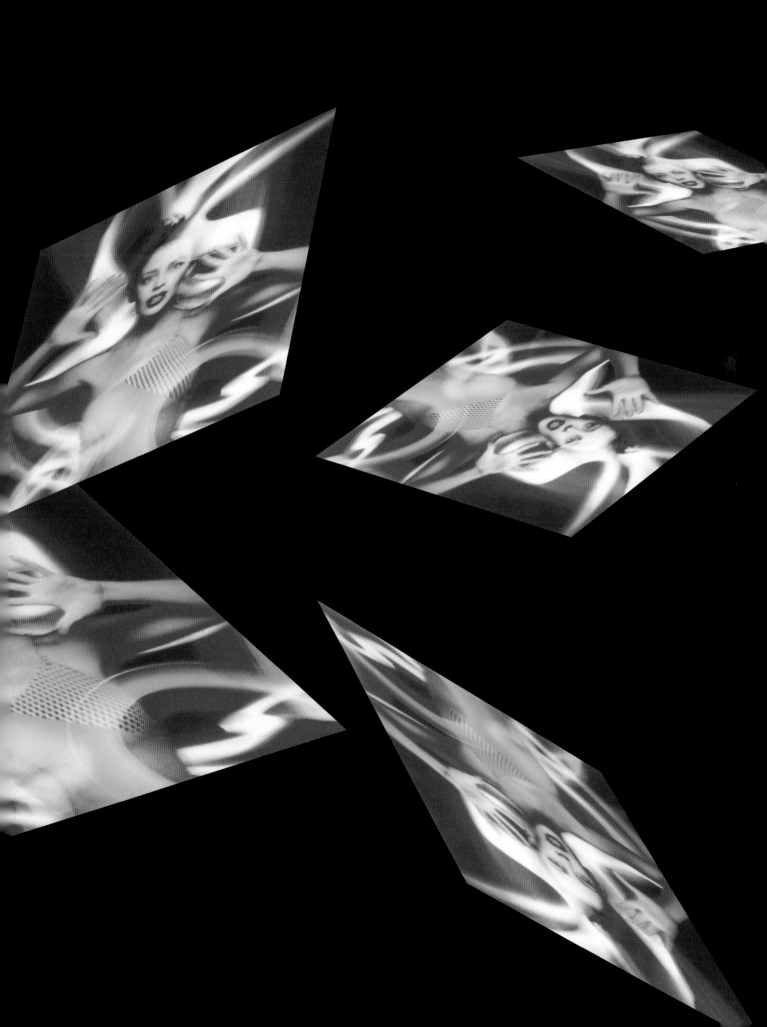

At first this was comical but after four days the joke began to wear off. Kylie had tired of sitting motionless as she waited for the long exposure to capture the image perfectly. The lights did look incredible on film and many thought that they were a post-production effect. This interminable shoot also featured painted backdrops of landscapes ranging from a fairy-tale castle to a contemporary cityscape skyline for Kylie to pose before: the kingdoms of an impossible princess.

It seemed that events conspired against *Impossible Princess*, and Princess Diana's terrible death a week before its release meant that radio stations abandoned pop for more sombre musical soundtracks, and it was decided out of respect to re-christen the album without the Princess reference. It became her third eponymous album, named simply *Kylie Minogue*, the same title as her previous deConstruction album, although it retained its original name in Australia. The release date was pushed back and back and it finally went on sale the following March, six months later.

Pete Hadfield commentated recently:

'There is a theory which was revealed to me recently that if she hadn't made the mistakes on the album, she wouldn't have come up with a return to pop genius. But she was between a creative rock and a hard place. Stephane was incredibly involved in the album, and she had me on the other end pulling in a different direction, and then it wasn't helped that I became seriously ill for around a year. So the creative direction didn't become so much muddled as compromised. We could have made a cohesive album because her ideas were magnificent. She was willing to take on musical genres that no one would have even expected her to consider. I regard it as a creative success, but creative successes aren't always commercial successes.'

Many of Kylie's fans still regard *Impossible Princess* as their favourite album, a sentiment shared by many who worked with her, but it remains the least successful release of her career. In hindsight, since Kylie's comeback, there has been a positive reassessment of the record: *Q* magazine named it one of the hidden gems of the nineties. Even at its release it was received rather well by the critics – but the public was not apparently willing to accept a darker, more serious Kylie.

The media hadn't helped matters with their depiction of Kylie during the making of the album. She was photographed leaving restaurants looking gaunt and pale, and rumours of eating disorders began to circulate. The papers ran articles asking what had gone wrong, saying that the 1998 Kylie was a shadow of her former self. Eating disorders couldn't have been further from the truth. The fact was that she had put her all into the making of the record. The studio sessions often stretched late into the night, and Kylie would then go and meet Stephane for a late supper. A paparazzi would invariably be lying in wait outside and pounce the moment that the couple would emerge, capturing her exhaustion for posterity.

Of all of her albums it remains my personal favourite because it is the one that I think truly mirrors and captures the complex person that Kylie is and in which she is totally honest. The album's lacklustre chart performance did not have the devastating effect on Kylie that I'd feared it might. She seemed content to have let it all out, and was ready to move on. Unlike those who thought that Kylie's career had been relegated to the bargain bins and was pretty much over now, she did not see this stray commercial failure as the end and never contemplated quitting (as she had done in the past at the end of an album's promotional period). She was too strong for that now.

The move from deConstruction was mutually agreed. Kylie's future was uncertain but she and her manager Terry were confident that they'd find another welcome somewhere and were oblivious to any general feeling that Kylie was over, despite the enduring obsession of the tabloids.

She returned home to Australia where the record had been a resounding success, free from the ties of an English record contract and free from any relationship, having parted from Stephane a couple of months earlier. Australia opened its arms, delighted to have its homecoming queen back.

cover star: **kylie** photographed by **mark mattock** september 1997

THE NEXT ISSUE NO.168

i-D

©

i-DEAS, FASHION, CLUBS, MUSIC, PEOPLE

£2.20 US$5.75

09

9 770262 357006

CAN $6.95 FRANCS 38 LIRE 9,700 DM 14,90 PESETAS 625 D KR 59

next...

07

: Intimate
and
live

189-207

Steve Anderson and I sat with guitarist Carl Mann and percussionist James Mack in a transit lounge at Dubai airport, trying to pass the tedium of a three-hour stopover by getting rat-arsed, while feeling slightly apprehensive about what lay ahead. It was May 1998 and we were en route to Australia for a two-month ten-date tour but neither Steve nor I knew quite what we were supposed to be doing, both of us virgins to the world of touring. Little did we know that we would spend the next five years trying to recapture the energy, enthusiasm, atmosphere and innocent joy of that tour.

Steve had been to Australia a couple of months earlier to arrange the music for Kylie's appearance at the twentieth anniversary Sydney Lesbian and Gay Mardi Gras, but it was my first time on the road, and I had no idea what to expect. By the time rehearsals began in Fitzroy, near Melbourne, the tour had been extended to twenty-four dates due to unprecedented demand. There was a tremendous buzz about Kylie in Australia, none of the cold-shouldering and indifference that had greeted *Impossible Princess* back in England. *Impossible Princess* did very well in the album charts there. Kylie was understandably sentimental about her homeland and couldn't wait to get back. Even those in her entourage, like us, were received like royalty as Kylie was regarded as one of the country's most successful ambassadors.

Australia's response to the celebrity of its own is usually defined by Tall Poppy Syndrome wherein the tallest flowers are cut down to size in the tabloids and gossip magazines. Kylie had become one of Australia's tallest poppies and had frequently been on the receiving end of their scorn, but this time it seemed like the whole country applauded their Impossible Princess's return. At the Adelaide Cup one day during rehearsals it might have been Royal Ascot as Kylie, every inch a princess, waved to adoring crowds. It was champagne, private jets and limos all the way. Melbourne's premier, Jeff Kennet, held a civic reception for her. Steve, Kylie and I took to it with the excitement of three newly-weds. The entire country seemed thrilled to have her back.

Kylie had toured before with her Let's Get To It, Rhythm Of Love and Enjoy Yourself shows and they had all been sell-out productions, but there was something special and unique about Intimate and Live, a coming-of-age for Kylie and her team. As never before she would excel as a live performer, the wonderfully supportive, honed and experienced teamwork enabling her to shine on stage like a true star.

Kylie was determined to take some risks on this tour - her journey of self-discovery during *Impossible Princess* had made her strong and confident enough to do so. She had re-established herself as a modern and formidable pin-up with the Hennes advertisements shot by Ellen Von Unwerth, despite the fact that some people had disliked the short hair and 'indie' look of *Impossible Princess*. The ads featured a smiley, relaxed nymphette, in marked contrast to the gritty black-and-white portrait that had graced the cover of 'Some Kind Of Bliss' only a few months earlier.

Smiley Kylie was back. Even in Britain, at the lowest point of her career and despite slow record sales, Kylie's popularity was evidenced by the fact that Madame Tussaud's decided to update their waxwork of her - a sure barometer of enduring public affection - replacing the original, with its yellow teeth and chipped nails, with a newly glamorous model, dressed in slinky Collette Dinnigan. I

wanted to make the original into a candle, but alas, Kylie was having none of it.

The power of Kylie's image endured. From rock chick to disco diva, from sex symbol to artist's muse, her image and celebrity status had kept her in the public eye despite having no discernable product of her own to promote. It enabled us to publish a book that we began later in the year after Intimate and Live, a project born out of sheer boredom and the need for a new challenge. *Kylie: Evidence* was in many ways emblematic of those wilderness years and attempted to gather a collection of various artists' perceptions of what Kylie meant to them.

We, frankly, couldn't figure out what these perceptions would be. Kylie as a public persona had so many different forms or guises: 'pop star, actress, sex siren, cover girl, soap star, singing budgie, pint-sized pop puppet, disco diva, pop princess, pocket Venus, control freak, part-time exhibitionist, alien, show pony, show-off, dancing queen, drag queen, artist or blank canvas?' The book, like everything else we did then, attempted to reconcile these split personalities of a girl who is a typical triple Gemini, with as many personalities or faces as a town hall clock. But instead of continually fighting against Kylie's pop schizophrenia, we decided to embrace it. The super eclectic show Intimate and Live brought this explosion of image and personas to the fore.

Kylie and I had brainstormed the design for the Intimate and Live stage set, scribbling concept drawings down onto a paper napkin for posterity. We had wanted a show that was built largely around the imagery of *Impossible Princess*, but which would take the audience on a journey and tease them with the unexpected, playing with their preconceptions. Most of all it would be a celebration of all things Kylie. By this point we were past caring what anyone else thought and Kylie, post lyrical exorcism on *Impossible Princess*, just wanted to lighten up and have fun.

Steve, Kylie and I were almost liberated by the British commercial failure of *Impossible Princess*, feeling that now we had nothing to lose. For this tour we could do exactly as we pleased.

We were so out of sorts with our post tour emptiness that we gave ourselves a new project, the book. Little did we know it would take 14 months, a lot of introspection and a lot of hard work. It is interesting now in retrospect to read into the more important reasons why we embarked on such a venture. I had lost objectivity and confidence as to who I was expected to be. How was I perceived in the public eye? Where was I to go from here? As it turned out we made a very creative and somewhat brave book exploring the media manifestations of a person. Each contributor had a page to do what they liked ... what does 'Kylie' mean to you? The results were interesting, inspiring and some of them to this day make no sense to me whatsoever ...

viewer to come closer and
e in Kylie's glittering
asy. The birth of this
girl cannot be pinpointed to
exact time or influence, but
most else with Kylie, it
ved and became part of her
e, in terms of both image and
ormance. The pin-up had
nally been devised to
brate extremely eroticised
es of beautiful women in
ographs and illustration. Its
larity grew as it captured a
n of impossibly perfected
ty. Kylie could always filter
look of the moment, whether
as the grunge of heroin chic,
he hi-camp of glamour,
ugh poise and posing.
he pin-up and her flesh-and-
d sister, the showgirl, were
ral to the development of
mate and Live and have been
gral to the Kylie ethos ever
e, reaching its most potent
ession in Kylie's role as the
n fairy Absinthe in Baz
mann's *Moulin Rouge*. By
cidence Baz attended the
mate and Live Show In Sydney
was transfixed by Kylie's
girl persona and performance.
rtunately for us, with the
girl came her elaborate,
-to-shimmy costumes and
ts, with the endless hours
eading and sequin festooning
helped bring them to life.
one corset that featured at
Sydney Lesbian and Gay Mardi
, my glamorous assistant Lucy
I worked into the night for
e weeks gluing each tiny red
anté in place by hand. We
so high on the fumes of the
rglue that the hours quickly
by.

Themes and images had been established at the London photo shoot for the tour programme. Photographer Simon Emmett had been inspired by Sam Hoskins' book *Cowboy Kate*. Full of energy, life and a natural glamour, these seventies images with their girly vitality seemed a perfect reference for Kylie. We devised some beautiful black-and-white images of her in Monroe mode and we achieved the Cowgirl look with the help of a Stephen Jones silver cowboy hat and Gucci leather bra combined with an old pair of burgundy Farrah's from a mod shop on Carnaby Street that we had made into pedal pushers.

We plundered Kylie's own cupboards for more props. Her favourite disco shoes were unearthed, an old sequinned Brazilian stripper's bikini and boob tube were all called into service and shot against backdrops of glitter stuck on wallpaper, beaded blinds and lengths of sequinned fabric and glitzy curtains.

we went pink and proud at a time when anything glittery and girly was decidedly uncool.

On our own and free from record company constraints we unashamedly revelled in what we loved and wanted, and the results of that shoot are some of our favourite and most iconic images.

GOES WITH
DISC 3

"0966 131 907."
karen.

SE-98-8-2

DIFFUSE + KEEP MOODY.
TRY 1 WITH RED WASH

frame 17

SE-98-8-19

DIFFUSE.

frame 18

SE-98-8-10

frame 11

frame 54

SE-98-8-21

frame 18

SE-98-8-13

frame 46

SE-98-8-21

frame 41.

frame 12

SHOT WITH

from DISC3

REF: KYLIE.

MIKE

all 12x10 as follows:

SE-98-8-8
frame 10.

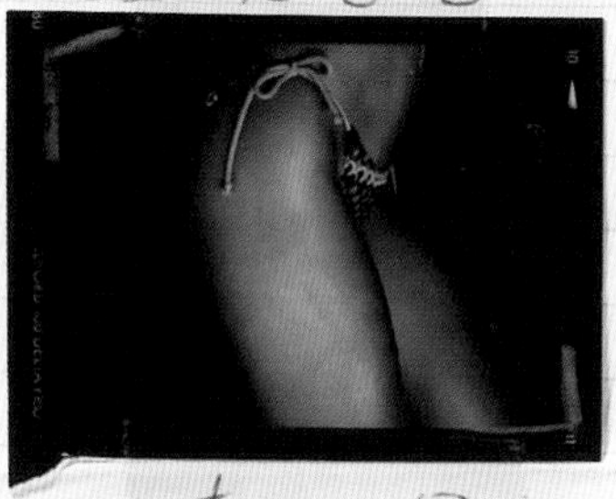

← PRINT LE[...]
BUT LIGH[...]

THIS ONE 
D8
frame 16   SE-98-8-6

SE-98-8-5
frame 12

SE-98-8-1 
frame 5

frame 15.   SE-98-8-9

SE-98-8-4 
frame 13.

D8.
Contact Sheet
removed.

MIRROR BALL. - STICK ON.

The show featured the John Farnham Band, with musical arrangements by Steve and Chong Lim, who had worked with Kylie at the grand opening of Melbourne's huge casino complex a couple of months earlier, when she had emerged in a puff of smoke out of a huge gleaming clam shell. The band were and remain paragons of Ozzie pub rock, as much a part of Ozzie culture as the barbie, and their participation symbolised the native authenticity of this tour.

Steve, Kylie and myself came up with the running order, which was largely based around *Impossible Princess* and included two songs which had been demoed but not released, 'Take Me With You' and 'Free'. The songs of Abba had been revived in Australia with the resounding international success of camp movies *Priscilla, Queen of the Desert* and *Muriel's Wedding*, each featuring songs by the sublime Swedes, and 'Dancing Queen' seemed the perfect choice for a homecoming queen now. I had always found the song to be somewhat melancholic, a sweeping and grandiose epitaph to the golden days of disco, with its connotations of the isolated showgirl of the title alone on a dance-floor.

The other cover was of The Clash's 'Should I Stay Or Should I Go?' which Kylie had recently performed on the Jonathan Ross TV show. 'The Locomotion' was added on the road when the audience decided they were going to sing it anyway, whether Kylie performed it or not.

Kylie and I always wanted the show to be very personal, a huge thank you to her fans, hence the 'Intimate' of the title. The venues were all small theatres, often with around a two thousand capacity, to enable bonding with her audience. Actually, at some dark and insecure moments in the planning, we had been worried about filling even those.

We had a shoestring budget to produce Intimate and Live and we all stretched the limits of improvisation. Those years of being brought up on a twice-weekly diet of *Blue Peter* finally paid off as everybody mucked in cheerfully. Kylie endeared herself to every member of the crew with her usual charm and courtesy. Under the guidance of tour manager Nick Pitts, who had toured extensively with Elton John, the assembled team put their all into making the tour one of the high spots of the careers of just about everybody involved.

The set was a sparse and simple affair, consisting of risers for the band and a central podium which interpreted and simplified a Las Vegas version of an Aztec temple. The cover imagery of *Impossible Princess*, which featured Kylie seated in a cone of multi-coloured light, was the inspiration for the show's opening and we recreated the light cone using a metal frame and strips of coloured translucent lycra stretched over it, teasing the audience first with a silhouette and then revolving it to reveal Kylie.

The Minogue manifesto clearly states that no Kylie show would ever be complete without a staircase, and we wanted the steps to light up as she walked down. This staircase was housed in the temple structure and was pushed forward through the temple doors by two stagehands, as we couldn't afford an electrical one. It seemed to have a mind of its own. Sometimes it would appear on cue and other nights fail to appear at all, leaving Kylie stranded on the platform above.

For a set piece for 'Confide In Me' at the end of the show, it was decided that Kylie should be revealed reclining on the stairs. Every night the doors would open and the staircase would rumble outwards with all the finesse of a door slamming on a wobbly *Neighbours* set, displaying Kylie perched on the stairs doing her best to look graceful whilst preventing the audience from seeing up her pistachio-green dress and at the same time trying not to hit her head on the ceiling of the platform. She looked like Kermit the Frog's cousin Robin.

Handwritten notes (top left):

silver
w perspex
lighting up
different
colour

filmed images - simple / stove ll

- eyes blinking
- lips ~~tq~~ licking. laughing (TOO FAR)

- driving in the desert.. (three)

photocopying

Take me with yu -

showgirns

PORNO section   more strippers
more porno images . silhouettes   see book ⬧

Step back - glitter ball

Take me with yu : elements
water, earth, sky, fire
exotic fruit   pyrotechnics

Kylie and I designed the costumes ourselves. The showgirl ensemble was the first one in place. A young fashion designer called Susanna Burgess, the girlfriend of a close friend of mine, made the costumes for us, unaware of how long sewing endless strips of sequins would take. After six weeks of going cross-eyed from relentless stitching, the costumes still weren't ready and were dispatched to Kylie's mum Carol and her nan – whom Kylie calls 'Nain', the Welsh word for 'grandmother' – to be finished. The pink striped corset dress was finished off with a matching ostrich-feathered showgirl tiara, beautifully handmade by Melbourne milliner Philip Rhodes. Indie Kylie's outfit from the 'Did It Again' video was reproduced in black for the show's opening, the jacket's clean lines emphasised by rows of jet bugle beads, again sewn by Kylie's mum and nan.

We had wanted a slim-line modern silhouette for the opening reveal through the lycra, but after the power pack for Kylie's ear monitors had been attached to the waistband of the pedal pushers Kylie thought her silhouette looked more like that

The audition process was a total revelation to me as I'd never been in this situation before. I sat behind a desk and sifted through piles of mug shots, all inanely grinning 'book me, book me', but bearing no resemblance to the gaggle of slick young twirlies that pranced around before us. They groaned as William, in full Lydia from *Fame* mode, and echoing her sentiments of 'Fame costs and here's where you start payin'!', asked them to remove their tops. They became suddenly sheepish, none of them able to look either of us in the eye.

Kylie sauntered in halfway through the proceedings and we sat like two giggling teenage girls slightly embarrassed to be in this position of authority. I knew exactly what we were looking for as I had an image of two bovver boys with lace-up Docs in my mind's eye, to give the show a deliberate fabulous bathhouse camp. We wanted them to look like

We were two costumes down and rescue came from Melbourne fashion designer Mark Burnett who has a successful label called Princess Highway. Mark, a devout disciple of eighties bad taste, worked in a studio above a cake shop on Melbourne's Chapel Street which Kylie and I frequented. We were often in stitches there as Mark delivered outrageous one-liners in a broad Ozzie drawl larded with 'ocker' phrases such as 'grouse' - Melbourne slang for anything that was good. With a constant background soundtrack of eighties Hi-NRG, from Divine to Sinitta, Mark's designs for Princess Highway reinterpreted the more tasteless trends of eighties fashion into something only slightly more tasteful yet somehow chic, this made all the more humorous by his insistence on modelling them himself.

He obsessed about dressing Kylie in an upside-down pineapple dress, only for her to point out that she had worn one years before. He was more persuasive with a design that he had typically christened a 'dead bird' top, describing a coiled trim of pleated hot pink chiffon that he piled onto the shoulder of an asymmetric clashing top.

Mark finally delivered Kylie's 'Cowboy Style' dress, a midnight blue saloon number festooned with his beloved sequin appliqués along the top of the bustier and cut into strips along the bottom. His corset for 'Better The Devil You Know' was totally covered in sequin appliqués which would rip into Kylie's armpits and was so tight she could hardly move.

Melbourne fancy-dress costumier Rose Chong, who resembled Zandra Rhodes with her strands of brightly dyed hair, made the boys' costumes. For 'Dancing Queen' she made hot pants detailed with the same sequin strips that decorated Kylie's corset. These were paired with two huge pink ostrich feather fans attached to a chest harness which every night Carol and I, with the aid of a hot glue gun, stuck further diamantés onto, not just too precious and obstinate to give in and buy the diamantés on a strip but actually preferring the *Blue Peter* couture approach.

The 'Cowboy Style' outfits were equally camp. The sex shop in New York that had so captivated us with its display of penis pumps had also supplied us with a bunch of G-string posing pouches embroidered with a dollar motif and stuffed with fake dollar bills. Kylie, after baring her bottom in Galliano's black net bus conductor homage on the last tour, sympathised with the dancers who weren't happy about exposing their rears, especially through a pair of teddy bear fur chaps, so Rose quickly turned the G-strings into Speedos which would disappear into their arses anyway as soon as they started dancing - so the desired effect was achieved.

For the more frenetic and darker number 'Limbo', we decided on black bondage trousers and straitjackets and for 'Devil', white tasselled trousers and red devil horns, which were mimicked by just about everybody in the audience.

Once the tour was up and running I began my two-month slavery to the quick change. There were six costume changes in the show and we had under a minute to get Kylie out of one and into another. Steve now devises the whole musical score for our tours around the timings of these hellish few seconds. Kylie would burst into the metre-square cubby-hole sending her PA Natalie Stevenson, mum Carol, hair and make-up man Kevin Murphy and me into total flapping panic.

Every night we would try to impose some kind of order, attempting to organise the removal of first her shoes, then her trousers, then her top, then her bra etc., but it never worked and always descended into chaos. Kevin would attempt to seize his moment and retouch Kylie's dripping visage or re-fix rebellious strands of hair that had escaped his glue-like hairspray as we all lunged for Kylie as if we were taming some wild, marauding beast. It was like the frantic activity portrayed in cartoons as a whirling cloud of smoke, out of which would fly various garments of Kylie's stage wardrobe.

I was often a quick change casualty, a victim of an accidental Manolo in the eye or a fist in my face. Things were made no easier by Carol and me being short-sighted (or usually a little worse for wear by then). I would forget my glasses and would fumble around in the darkness, like Thelma from *Scooby-Doo*, trying to find one of the hideous pop socks Kylie insisted on wearing inside her boots. One night we forgot to fasten the catch on her cowgirl dress and watched in horror from the wings as the dress began to slip down under the weight of her power pack. Down it went, further and further down her chest whilst I chain-smoked and Carol swigged Chardonnay furiously, flapping our arms around like demented traffic controllers trying to catch her attention, though careful not to spill our *vino* at the same time. Natalie ran to the rescue, braving the crowds and fastening the catch, the thought of running on stage absolutely horrifying to Carol and me.

We skulked back to our makeshift booth where Kevin immediately handed us another drink to calm our nerves. We were frequently sozzled by the end of the show, having had our first glass as we sent Kylie on her way, our own version of smashing a champagne bottle against the side of a ship. We wished her *bon voyage* each night, then legged it to catering where Kevin would have a bottle, a corkscrew and four glasses at the ready. We would then time ourselves to a glass for every two sections of the show. Carol got so tipsy one night she allowed us to dress her up as Baby Spice.

The tour ended and our bubble burst. A roadie, concerned about our long faces, informed us that in America they had rehab clinics for people who spent their lives on the road and struggled to integrate back into a normal existence. Suffering from an extreme bout of post-tour depression, Kylie and I contemplated calling International Enquiries for the number, but that was as far as it got. Perhaps we should have gone into therapy at that point. We returned to England with an unavoidable feeling of emptiness. We seemed so far away from the adoring crowds and nightly highs. But three shows at London's Shepherd's Bush Empire finished the tour in triumphant fashion and provided a short fix, receiving rave reviews and perhaps slightly altering London's perception that Kylie was over.

Crowd response to the Intimate and Live tour had indicated above all else that Kylie was a pop icon and was loved for her interpretations of pop songs. 'Better The Devil You Know' and 'Dancing Queen' were without doubt the favourite numbers of the show and pointed in the direction she should follow if she wanted to make another album: a return to her pop disco roots.

The 'tour bubble' is a weird and wonderful place.

PICTURE EXCLUSIVE

Who's this
cheeky star?

A **REAR-LY** lovely singer airs her greatest bits at a concert . . . but who is she?

The beauty stunned fans with a skimpy outfit and raunchy routine. Here's a clue — we've *been* seen of her lately. To get to the bottom of it *turn to* Page Seven! Picture: NIKOS/EQUINOX

209-227

By the time I signed with Parlophone in 1999
I was ready to start afresh: new label, new
record, new appreciation for my strengths
and awareness of my weaknesses and of
what my audience wanted. Pop, it seemed,
was not a dirty word. We were all ready to
embrace it and not just hand the public
what they wanted but to present the
ingredients they know in an even more
exaggerated form. 'Light Years' was unashamed.
I figured I had given the experimental route
my best shot and had gained so much from
the experience. Now I would take a different tack
at full speed. I was definitely ready for
something fun. Key words for 'Light Years' were
poolside, disco, cocktails, beach and loveboat.
A cruiseship where you could set your cares
aside and kick your heels up with gay abandon.
All of the writers and producers, including the
formidable team of Robbie Williams and Guy
Chambers, came on board with great enthusiasm.
They all had the benefit of hindsight and an
objective perspective on the 'I.F.' years and all
agreed that it was actually very simple. With
the right songs I would be back in the charts.
The bottom line was pop. Pop it was, and
the bottom line took on a whole new meaning.

I never liked 'Spinning Around'. I heard the song for the first time sitting at the breakfast bar in Kylie's kitchen. Kylie was playing me some select cuts from the songs she had recently demoed for her forthcoming album – she often gives her friends tasters of what is to come and she listens to their varied responses, it helps her clarify her own thoughts and feelings. The song I listened to, dominated by a hideous Status Quo-style guitar riff in the middle eight, was different from the released version. There was something distinctly un-Kylie about the song and arrangement. Plenty of other songs on the album demo seemed to be more obvious hits. We were all aware that the next single was crucial for Kylie, and we were all anxious to get it right. A flop would have almost certainly meant the end of a pop career for her. 'Spinning Around' stood out as a song that was distinctly American in its style. It would have been perfect for Paula Abdul, who wrote it, or even Mariah Carey, for example, but for Kylie?

I was proved wrong and forced to eat my Philip Treacy hat. 'Spinning Around' was a runaway hit. Parlophone's vision triumphantly reintroduced Kylie back to the masses. Their choice of single, with its heady declarations of female strength and renewal, made it in their eyes the perfect comeback anthem and the modern filtered disco twang provided an irresistible chorus that would appeal to a wide audience. I still don't like it though.

When Kylie signed to Parlophone her already established team stayed in place. Manager Terry Blamey and the creative team – myself, graphic designer Mark Farrow and Steve Anderson – were all engaged in yet another regeneration. The A&R direction led by Keith Wozencroft, Miles Leonard and Jamie Nelson was and is particularly strong, as they insisted from the outset that what they wanted to do was make pop records for a pop audience.

They weren't too bothered about building on the Kylie ethos that already existed, preferring instead a fresh start, to wipe the slate clean. The charts were again bombarded with manufactured pop and again overrun with rampaging pre-pubescent girlies. Early nightmares were that they wanted to make Kylie into a cross between Billie and Lolly but thankfully their vision was a lot more refined.

Mark Farrow wanted the marketing that would accompany the Parlophone debut to be based around a fashion campaign, upon concepts of branding. Post Spice Girls pop was enjoying an unprecedented period of branding. Each Spice Girl had represented something different to the consumer and in buying into the Spice concept the audience could participate with the band and implied lifestyles, the one chosen depending very much on which was the favourite Spice. Pop was at its most interactive.

Fashion advertisements and the lifestyle options they offer are also interactive, offering participation in the product, a philosophy based around a concept of envy. Fashion advertisements offer, like pop stars, escapism.

Stella McCartney's Chloé was a perfect example of branding in fashion and inspired the styling and creative direction of 'Spinning Around'. Stella offered a tantalising world of blonde, tanned, sexy vitality mixed with hints of west London ragga chic. The Chloé girl, personified in Stella's then design assistant Phoebe Philo, who was a long-time friend of mine, was liberated and confident, trilby at the ready, a girl-woman. The mirrored sunglasses with diamanté heart appliqué subsequently became the summer's must-have item, combined with seventies-style airbrushed baseball shirts and vests depicting anything from sunsets to hummingbirds. There was a strong disco element to their designs, creating a look and ethos akin to one of a refined Roller Girl.

The Chloé philosophy that season was the embodiment of what Kylie represented and what we wanted to project. The photographer behind the Chloé campaigns was Liz Collins and it was apparent that these images were produced for women by women who simply revelled in the joy of being women. Liz Collins' photographs of Kylie, the most famous being the pink hula-hoop image for the cover of 'Spinning Around', were everything we wanted them to be: fresh, natural and glamorous.

The make-up was a tanned beach glow with a gloss applied to eyelids and the lips and freckles were added and emphasised with a chocolate eyeliner, the hair loosely tousled. The pictures brought out Kylie's natural sunshine and epitomised her new *raison d'être*: fun. The imagery signified the triumphant return of Kylie as the girl-next-door who had grown up, and become a woman.

I delight in being a woman with all its contradictions. It's the only way to truly be myself. It's sometimes hard to be considered a 'whole' person when most people are only privy to a two-dimensional version of me.

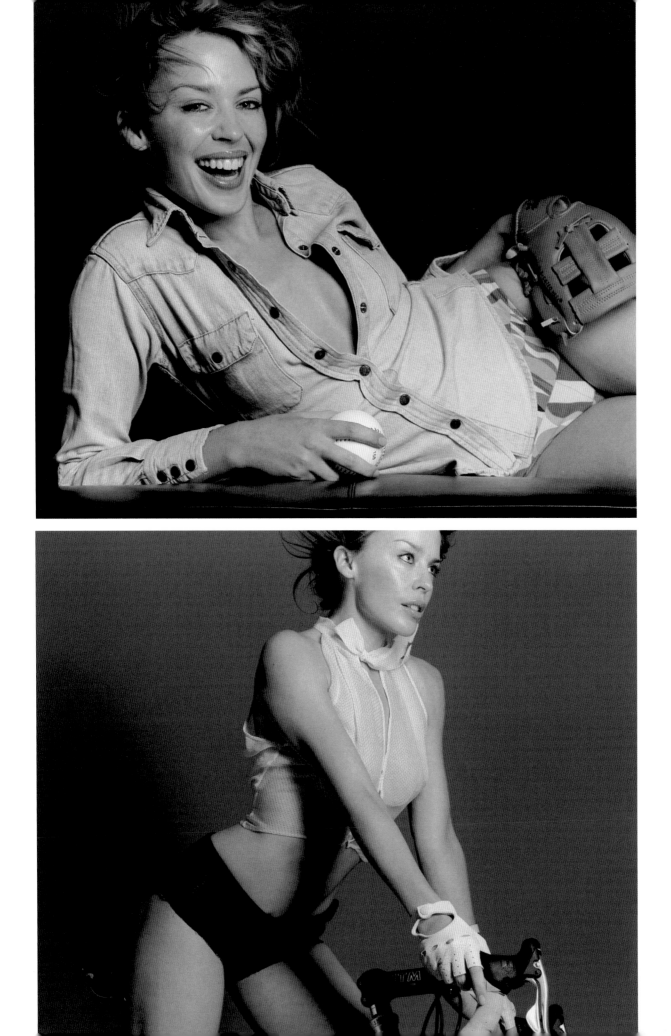

The director of the accompanying clip for 'Spinning Around' was also a woman, Dawn Shadforth. Her video provided a contrast to the voyeurism often evident in male directors' work, as in 'Put Yourself In My Place', for example, wherein the viewer is given a fly-on-the-wall perspective as space vixen Minogue's hot pink spacesuit is lifted from her body by the gravitational void of deep space. The sexiness that Dawn captures in Kylie is delicately different in that it offers the viewer participation. As a woman, she knows what women find attractive, confident in her own sexuality, and offers a much more rounded performance than those directed by and immortalised by men, who have a tendency to interpret Kylie as an image stereotype, a projection and manifestation of male fantasy.

I had previously worked with Dawn, a sexy Sheffield lass with a big heart, as a stylist on Garbage's video for 'Special', and Geri Halliwell's 'Bag It Up'. Dawn's love of pop and glamour and appreciation of the female power icon is evident in all her work with female pop stars, endowing all her subjects with the aura of a goddess.

Her sense of humour and irony are integral to her work. I think she is simply the best pop video director around. Her experience of directing underground dance artists provides her poppier subjects with an immediate edge as she pushes back the boundaries of established artists' existing myths and personas.

She presented Shirley Manson as a gorgeous space fighter pilot blasting her male band members out of the stars, with a comic-book sexiness emphasised by erotic cutaway details: the legs revealed through a camouflage leather miniskirt, the booted feet on the pedals of her spacecraft, the grip of her gloved hand on the controls; shots that she repeated later for Kylie driving her custard-yellow car in 'Can't Get You Out Of My Head'.

Influenced by fashion photography, she bestows on her subjects a contemporary allure and glamour, often favouring airbrushed images of perfection. Dawn loves glossy lips and pale flesh. Geri was presented as a catsuited superheroine-cum-mad scientist, creator of Girl Power, which transforms males into sex slaves of the female.

Dawn empowers women, bringing out their sensuality and combining it with a humour that is not confrontational, merely sexy. Working with Kylie was an ambition fulfilled and Dawn allows those with whom she works to do what they excel at and enjoy most within the context of the world her films create. Kylie likewise knows that collaborations work best when each participant is allowed self expression, even if this is through her, the star. By encouraging this creative freedom, both obtain results that would be impossible under controlling direction, often unimaginably better. Kylie summed it up: 'It is a case of one plus one equals three.'

Working with Dawn is always fun and tremendously rewarding. The shoot for 'Spinning Around' was hilarious and very upbeat. Juicy Lucy and Richard, my assistants, were dispatched to Camden and Portobello markets and designer press offices to gather clothes for the numerous extras who resembled a cross between a latter-day Studio 54 crowd and American trailer trash kids.

Knowing Dawn's penchant for calling for extra extras, Juicy and Dicko plundered their own wardrobes due to our restricted costume budget, and subsequently created marvellous ensembles to dress the ever multiplying crowd. Dressing the extras on videos is as important as dressing the star: the frame around the artist is intrinsic to creating the right ambience. A number of roller-skaters glided around the shoot looking fantastic, yet they are barely noticeable in the final result.

For Kylie's costume, I was keen to continue the Chloé reference and they provided the white denim hot pants and gold chain top which she wears in the finished version, as well as the knitted gold bikini she wears on the fibre-optic bed. The slashed red number came from Alexander McQueen. Then, of course, there were the gold hot pants...

The story of the hot pants has already become pop legend; one rumour had it they cost fifty pence and came from Oxfam. First unearthed by Kat at a market somewhere for a ridiculously low price (Kat is always discovering hidden treasures at thrift stores or markets), they resided comfortably amidst the slingshot swimming costumes, nipple tassels and Brazilian thongs in one of Kylie's many bottomless drawers. Their first official appearance was at a Rankin photo shoot for *Kylie Ultra*, her website for a feature named 'Dress Kylie', in which the user could dress Kylie in an outfit of choice, from a nurse's uniform, through a maid's outfit accessorised with a kettle or a hairdryer, to a white trash look involving the gold lamé shorts.

Their next outing was for a party that Kylie attended with Stephane. The theme was Tarts, Nerds and Tourists. Kylie, naturally, went as a tart and Stephane as a pervy tourist. One of Kylie's old PWL wigs came out of another drawer and the photographic proof is in *Kylie: Evidence*. The night before the video shoot I went to Kylie's house to see what delights Kylie's wardrobe could supply. Under a pile of transit lingerie were the steaming ruby hot pants.

Dawn loved them, they clung perfectly to every curve of Kylie's cheeky, peach-like bottom. Matched with the Chloé top and gold Gina stilettos, with make-up by Mary Jane Frost and a modern-day Farrah Fawcett flick, courtesy of Malcolm Edwards, the look fitted perfectly into the chic seventies *Wallpaper*-style disco that the art department had created in the studio.

The golden tones of Kylie's outfit, skin and hair complemented the wood and glass veneer of the interior. Kylie spent every minute of the two-day shoot worrying about the pants disappearing into her cheeks and I was on the lookout to make sure everything remained in place for the sliding down the bar scene.

I was so self-conscious in the minuscule hotpants, it was fortunate I wasn't aware the camera was so snugly trained around my posterior.

By the end of the shoot, after so much sliding and grinding, most of the lamé had worn off the fifty-pence wonders, revealing two perfect circles of the white fabric base on the butt cheeks. They took up a brief residency at the Barbican's Rock and Fashion exhibition for three months before flying to Australia, where Carol keeps an eagle-eyed vigil over many of her daughter's stage ensembles hanging mothballed in a Melbourne storage vault.

Recreating the originals was impossible, although we made several attempts to reprise their glory for promotions around the country, eventually coming up with a tasselled pair. The mark two pants arrived two hours before Kylie was due on stage one night at the Astoria, and were so tight she couldn't even get them around her thigh. We had attempted to make them a little more 'secure' than the originals, lining them with stretch-power net to ensure a tight hold. The next two hours were spent with me in chain-smoking panic while Kylie unpicked certain seams and slashed the lining so she could inch them on. Once *in situ* there was no getting out of them except by dint of the scissors and we had to cut Kylie out in quick change mayhem.

Flirty and dangerous, the gold lamé hot pants became an emblem of Kylie's image – visually provocative, classically seductive and a simple fantasy, as their golden sheen, together with her bronzed skin and the deep blonde of her flicked hair, created and communicated luxury.

They became a national obsession, bestowing upon her bottom a celebrity all of its own. The tabloids recognised the selling power of the Minogue rear and there have probably been as many front pages devoted to her butt as to her face. The media began a game of spot the bum, counting how many times it wiggled during her Fever tour.

If Warhol were alive, her bottom would surely have been the subject of one of his portraits, inspired by repetition of image and mass-marketing of idols and icons. Her bum became an icon and the endless debate about it has developed a life of its very own.

Princess Julia, London DJ celebrity, social commentator and fashion junkie, observed that the hot pants are a covering - essential in the art of seduction. They represent a modern chastity belt in their minimal metallic sheen and the idea of a hidden prize, a golden fleece to be won, but securely locked away.

The pants reveal just enough flesh to tease but Kylie remains chaste, pure and untouched. This in itself is the secret of seduction. To remain out of reach, aloof and mythical. Like the chastity belt, they keep something locked away, and in the ensuing dance Kylie can tease and provoke, knowing she is safely in control.

The dance routine in the video was choreographed by Luca Tommasini, whom I'd also met doing time with Geri. Characterised by its infamous bum slap, it celebrated the Minogue ass. The routine was sensual, erotic and fun, essentially the kind of dance that could be picked up easily and reproduced at the school disco. Luca had the unenviable task of teaching the routine to a bunch of extras who weren't all professional dancers, providing hours of hilarity as they attempted to master and capture it. There were times when they were also required to dance freestyle, creating the natural ambience of a club. All of the dance scenes had to be cut around a very cute boy who sadly had about as much rhythm as a decomposing corpse. As he'd been placed next to Kylie the choice of shots of the dancing star was limited.

Prior to the video shoot I was in LA with my boyfriend, James Gooding. I had just bought a house there and had grand plans of lapping up the sunshine in relative obscurity in the States. James and I were having an incredible time, falling in love and running around, generally having fun and getting into desirable amounts of trouble. It was a time when I really didn't know what the future held and wasn't counting on being super successful, hence the house purchase in LA: a grown ups' playground. As it turned out the house was only graced by my presence twice and ended up back on the market because I didn't have any time to go there. Work started all over again in a bigger way then ever before. I was jet lagged for most of the shoot but was in a good frame of mind. In James I had found someone who helped me find a challenging and harmonious balance between work and the 'Kylie' people don't often see. We met at a time when I wasn't Kylie Incorporated, just me. He's been influential on my style and image, but his influence has been more profound in the world I sometimes find more challenging, the 'real' world. Harmony is now my constant aim.

The video proved immediately successful, from its beginning depicting Kylie's gold Gina heels walking slowly across the screen, a metaphor for her ongoing journey and continual process of transformation, through to its revealing portrait of the *derrière*, the bar sliding and eventual *Boogie Nights*-style joining-in on the dance-floor. The song entered the charts at Number One, providing Kylie with her fifth top slot, making her and Madonna the only artists to have Number One singles in the eighties, nineties and noughties.

Kylie was at a Sunday lunch at James's grandmother's house in the country when she received the call that she was back at the top of the charts for the first time in nearly ten years. She admits having to go outside where she shed a tear, called a few friends, then returned to her roast chicken. My phone rang. A tearful voice quivered quietly out of my mobile: 'Darling... we're Number One.'

Much was made of her comeback but to many it seemed like she had never been away. An omnipresent figure in the tabloids, her return had all the warm familiarity of a reunion with a little sister who had spent a summer InterRailing. The general consensus was that she had zipped up her boots and gone back to her roots, but this implied a defeatism at odds with Kylie's constantly evolving image and career. She moves in only one direction: forward. The last few years had been spent attempting to justify her popularity and appeal, trying to reconcile the complexities and disguises of her showbiz persona with Kylie Ann Minogue, the private, slightly eccentric girl from Melbourne, now thirty-one years of age. Kylie had put these troubles to bed.

'Have Pants, Will Travel' was the *Sun*'s immediate response to her return to the Number One slot. However, it was more than just those slithers of ruched gold lamé which adorned Miss Minogue's rear that took 'Spinning Around' to the top of the charts. The song was a battle cry against all those who over the past decade had their beady little eyes focused on her glistening tiara. With a metaphorical jab of her gold stilettos she declared, 'Did I forget to mention that I found a new direction? And it leads back to me...'

I felt so many emotions at the time... elation, vindication, surprise and relief. I repeatedly questioned the authenticity of the chart position I was being congratulated on by phone, convinced there had to be some kind of mistake and too nervous to let go and believe it after the #1 predictions throughout the week. I felt pleased and thankful for all of the people who had either worked on the project or who had stood by me during that busy period or difficult times.

I took a deep breath, shed a tear and went back to playing backgammon: my devised distraction from 'Sunday chart position' anxiety

Vincent Peters was selected to photograph Kylie for the cover of *Light Years*, the shoot taking place outside a villa at the far north of Ibiza Island. Vincent was selected because he wore tight T-shirts and jeans halfway down his Calvins, as well as for his extraordinary photographs. His images are instantly iconic, sleek and polished. He is the Helmut Newton of an era of technically generated and enhanced images. We wanted him to interpret Kylie in his unique, hyper-unreal style. The women he photographs are extraordinary creatures of fantasy, with elongated limbs, always posed in positions of dominance; he creates modern images of powerful women. He has said, 'I don't think that there would be any media if there wasn't a necessary illusion.'

With the image he created for *Light Years*, Kylie's presence is glorified against a backdrop of sky and sea, a glimpse of golden sunset filtering through and creating a supernatural halo around her. Kylie gazes towards some heaven, arm raised and frozen as if to point out something unrecognisable or cast a spell as she rests upon a liquid surface. The photograph is the perfect depiction of heavenly light, imbuing the image with an almost religious sensibility, enhanced by the deep blue of her garment. The sea in ancient mythology symbolises a woman's sexuality and something of Mary Magdalene is evoked by this temptress and siren calling passing sailors to her harbour and their doom. Here she is pop's Boadicea, triumphant and self-assured. She knows who she is and what she does best. As Vincent Peters puts it:

'The great thing about Kylie is how she differs from other celebrities. There is a separation between how the celebrity perceives themselves and what the public wants to see. Most are concerned with reproducing a certain logo or caricature of themselves. They want to cling on to an image developed years ago which makes things difficult because there is no room to take a picture, you aren't really forced to improvise which is when the best things happen. Every photographer has their own very personal vision of her, and she lets them have that. That is the big difference with Kylie, that she walks in and she says "This is me, what are you going to do with it?"'

Neil Rodgers, the stylist
formerly known as Jackie, was
lured out of retirement by the
promise of a free trip to Ibiza.
Costumes from Paris and Milan
were delivered to the ramshackle
Ibiza hotel that we shared with
the dancers who were performing
with Kylie at Manumission night
at the Privilege nightclub. By
day the dancers sunned themselves
in a glowing assortment of the
tightest and skimpiest Speedos
that would have given Club
Tropicana George Michael a run
for his money. The hotel couldn't
afford a beach and was sited on
what can only be described as a
rocky outcrop, so the dancers
risked life and limb for their
tans and every time they headed
for the sea that was crashing
below onto the jagged edges of
the coastline.

   A villa was hired, and Kylie
was looking forward to enjoying a
quiet rest in the lap of relative
luxury with James and her
brother, despite the mayhem of
her schedule. She gasped in pure,
poor-little-rich-girl horror when
she saw that the glorious, modern
location villa, the setting for
the *Light Years* shoot, with its
horizon swimming pool and one of
the island's most exclusive and
stunning views, was actually
occupied by the Parlophone
contingent. 'Bastards' was all
she could manage, as Miles, Jamie
and Jason Lamont came to greet
her after an arduous drive
through the winding mountain
roads.

   Never have so many clothes
been made from so little fabric.
We must have had a hundred
different bikinis, most of which
were tried on and discarded
before we settled on the Jeremy
Scott royal blue chiffon costume
featured in the finished image.
It arrived by courier only two
hours before the end of the shoot
so it was a race against time to
capture the glorious light
provided by the setting sun.

The video for Kylie's second single from *Light Years*, 'On A Night Like This', was shot in Monte Carlo. The director, Douglas Avery, was again inspired by fashion imagery and wished to create an atmosphere of wealth and luxury. Steven Miesel's campaign for Versace featured models with bouffants high enough to rival those of their poodle companions. He created a world of superpower and international hair not seen since the days of *Dynasty:* opulence, diamonds and champagne, limos, more diamonds and casinos. I was reliving my youth spent with the Carringtons all over again. Douglas based his script for the video on Martin Scorsese's film *Casino*, with its Las Vegas luxury concealing a sinister criminal underbelly of mafia control. I preferred to see it as a recreation of the 'lucky bitches' world of *Dynasty* but the same glamour element ran through the two.

Kylie's character was loosely based around that of the Sharon Stone role from the film, replacing her spectacular death from a barbiturate overdose in a perfect Pucci ensemble with an ambiguous demise in a swimming pool. Kylie spent a long night shoot dripping wet, either submerged in the pool or shivering between takes with only a towel and hot air from a hairdryer to keep her warm.

We had borrowed a gorgeous Versace multi-coloured dress from their press office. It apparently sold for about £4,000 in the stores. I omitted to tell them that the dress was going to be submerged in chlorinated water, then removed and chucked against a glass window. It was painstakingly altered for Kylie's diminutive frame, ensuring that the fabric was rolled and tucked rather than cut so the dress could still do the rounds of editorial shoots and be worn by models a size bigger. The two of us both held our breath during its submersion, fearing that the delicate printed lace could either disintegrate or shrink and land us with an enormous bill.

Fortunately the dress held out, but as I dried her off between takes with the hairdryer, the bottom chiffon layer shrank to about six inches short of the lace. The press office, grateful for the exposure, forgave us and didn't charge. Designer Roland Mouret, genius of the drape, was inspired by the glamour of such designers as Halston and Yves Saint Laurent and designed two of the other dresses Kylie wore for the video: a black silk jersey number encrusted with

Swarovski crystals, and a blue sequin halter neck she removes in true classy style in the back of a limo.

The dresses were accessorised with millions of dollars' worth of diamonds, borrowed from a jeweller in Monte Carlo. The jewels were simple and breathtakingly beautiful, the hugest white and yellow diamonds I had ever seen and Kylie, naturally, loved every minute of wearing them. With the diamonds came two enormous security guards that became our shadows, not leaving the jewels for a second and not allowing anyone, apart from Kylie, to touch them. Any hopes of Kylie slipping them into her clutch bag were immediately dashed.

I'd started doing hair and make-up, but the reflection looking back at me from the Winnebago mirror was decidedly plain. Then the diamonds arrived. I had never seen such huge jewels and I was wearing them in an instant. I was suddenly transformed and plain no more. I spent much of the night trying to wear the security men down. I managed to make one of them smile, but the other's steely gaze read 'you may be cute but you may also be a jewel thief!'

Disaster struck on the morning of the second day of shooting, when the jeweller informed us that the diamonds had been promised to some princess at a charity ball that evening in Dubai and we were unable to borrow them back for the completion of the shoot. The jewels were so ostentatious that only a blind man would fail to notice their absence and continuity is vital to retain any semblance of credibility in a video. Panic set in as I was forced to Sellotape two Berwick Street diamanté bracelets together and utilise the fake lookalikes that we had used on the extras. Fortunately these were only seen from a distance and continuity was preserved.

Rutger Hauer of *Blade Runner* and Guinness advert fame was chosen to be Kylie's sugar daddy or father in the 'story'. His presence lent a solemnity and gravitas to the proceedings, everyone slightly in awe of the formidable Dutch actor with his huge cowboy hat and desert boots. He did indeed supply the required air of menace to the video and the short film is beautifully shot and directed, even though to this day we still don't have the faintest clue as to what is going on.

For the promotion of the single we again borrowed the shrunken Versace dress, which had remained on the hanger of the press office because no one else apart from Kylie could now fit into it. Luca again created a memorable routine for the song featuring a group of Italian girl dancers who were as feisty as they were sexy. Dressed in Copperwheat Blundell jersey dresses and perched on four-inch silver stilettos, they sat on gold Louis XIV-style upholstered chairs which we had covered ourselves using several Versace scarves cut to shreds and velcro.

Every time the girls moved their legs the dresses would ride up, arched legs protruding from side-splits and we worried that it all might be a little much for Saturday morning television. Two other girls reclined on sheepskin rugs on either side of Kylie. She, with her love for anything tactile and furry, nicked the rugs for her apartment from whence they would resurface every now and again to cover her throne on the tour bus.

The third single from *Light Years* was a duet with Robbie Williams entitled 'Kids'. We had met Robbie years earlier the night after he performed with Take That for the last time at the Brit Awards. Kat had photographed Take That and I had tagged along, Kat and I being inseparable at the time. Robbie and I bonded, discovering our home towns were about ten miles apart up north. He was fun, flirty and obnoxious. He had a crush on Kylie and could never keep it together in front of her, then or now. He escaped from the Chelsea Harbour Hotel the night after the Brits and came over to Kylie's to watch the performance on TV. For *Light Years* he and his songwriting partner Guy Chambers composed three tunes, 'Love Boat', 'Your Disco Needs You' and 'Kids'.

Kylie and Robbie were an explosive combination and 'Kids' was a rousing pop rock anthem. The video in which they appear together was based around John Travolta and Olivia Newton-John in *Grease*, particularly 'You're The One That I Want'. Roland Mouret designed the tight black snakeskin pants that Kylie wore and the black jersey drape top, tied in a knot above her midriff. Kylie hated her hair in the video, describing it as resembling Darth Vader's helmet. Their on-screen chemistry was obvious, with Robbie and Kylie trying to out-flirt and out-camp each other.

Robbie's persona had a touch of the song and dance to it and Kylie's Ginger Rogers was the perfect partner for his Fred Astaire: their combination was hypnotic. The press had a field day, desperate for the nation's pop sweethearts to be caught in a real clinch offstage. Kylie was now on the front pages every week and the Robbie collaboration added fuel to her already blazing fire.

09
:
Loved
up
in
lamé

-
the
on
a night
like
this
tour

'To perceive camp in persons is to understand being as playing a role. It is the farthest extension of life as theatre.'
Susan Sontag

Kylie is undoubtedly most at home on the inside of the stage door. She simply loves performing. When the glare of the spotlight she glistens and gleams like a newly-cut diamond. Her performance and style owe as much to Hollywood, Busby Berkeley, the chorus cuties of the Moulin Rouge, the high-kicking lovelies of the New York Follies and the Folies Bergère as to the queens of modern pop.

She has the cheeky charm of the chorus line, is as smouldering as Veronica Lake, as vivacious as Rita Hayworth, as sexy as Mae West and as vulnerable as Marilyn Monroe. She has Debbie Harry's style, Madonna's chameleon instinct and Bette Midler's pizzazz. There is always wit in her performance, whether she enters the stage aboard a giant flip-flop, as she did at the Olympics opening ceremony, or marches down an illuminated staircase, flanked by fifty marching boys dressed as devils. Her performing tongue is firmly in her cheek.

The On A Night Like This tour grew out of *Light Years*, which in retrospect was a glorious powder puff of a record, as pink as Barbara Cartland, a glitter fest of all that shimmers, the perfect soundtrack to her nights all over the world and perfect musical wallpaper for any gay club, especially the ones with a talking carpet on the dance floor and poppers pumped through the air conditioning. The epitome of Kylie's pop perfection begins with a run of pure disco. Bubblegum beats, Motown hand claps and hooks galore. New York House and the disco-electronica of Georgio Moroder. It is a perfect slice of connoisseurs' disco.

The tour merchandise was emblazoned with a Hawaiian postcard, printed on everything from towels to T-shirts and bearing the slogan 'Greetings From Camp Kylie'. Camp it certainly was, from the copious amounts of glitter the make-up artist smeared on every visible part of Kylie's petite frame (and it usually ended up on parts that weren't visible) to the Italian Pierre et Gilles-style Gaultier-clad sailor boys who pranced around the decks of HMS *Kylie*.

Based on Bette Midler's early bathhouse days, it was pure burlesque. The Divine Miss M had been a heroine of both mine and Kylie's for years: she had always managed to capture and perfectly blend sexiness, bawdy slapstick and pure tack with the grace of a showgirl queen. Streisand took herself much too seriously for us. Give us mermaids in wheelchairs any day.

Hollywood musicals were also a key inspiration, particularly the maritime romps like *Anchors Away* and *South Pacific*. I also wanted some of Lola's devilish seductiveness from the fantastic *Damn Yankees*.

The show opened with the gleaming decks of *RMS Kylie* complete with sun loungers and a bamboo cocktail bar covered with pin-ups of sailors (apart from one night when the crew replaced them with pictures of readers' wives from a porno mag which catered for tastes in size eighteen and above) and Kylie descending from the painted clouds astride a huge glittering anchor and into a mass of sailors and hula girls cavorting around the deck with as much gay abandon as they could muster.

Musicals were the inspiration not just for the show's content but also for the design. The proscenium arch of an old deco theatre provided the perfect frame for such a carry-on. The set was simple: a stylised ramp or runway along the back wall divided underneath into sections for the band, which gave the whole proceedings a feel of *The Muppet Show*. The backdrops were painted gauzes displaying scenes from the ocean liner and various skies to a deco interpretation of the Broadway skyline and the 2001 starship interior that opened the encore.

. . . was constructed with separate . . . . . each with its own mini storyline and theme. . . . . . was 'Love Boat', featuring . . . . roller boys and hula girls . . . . . floral Hawaiian leis, ... garrotting them as . . . . snapping and . . . . deck with their . . . . lovers. Second was . . . . . . section comprising a . . . . Hi-NRG classics from . . . . . days and finishing with fan favourite anthem 'Your Disco Needs You'. There was a Broadway section, a club section featuring the more dance orientated . . . . , and finally a *Space Odyssey* section to showcase the Donna Summer electronica homage and title track of the album *Light Years*.

Greetings frm

CAMP KYLIE

SUMMER 2001

'Love Boat' featured an idyllic retro cruise ship, HMS *Kylie*, based on the sailing vessel from the seventies TV series that gave the song its name. The ocean liner set turned from day into night as it cruised imaginary tropical seas with the help of a starcloth concealed behind the gauzes where the clouds had been before. The cloth also featured heavily in the revue section, complete with a huge Kylie logo made of lights. The main inspiration for the eighties medley came from the baseball locker rooms of *Damn Yankees* and also from a Vegas show featuring showgirl dancers in American football armour. Culture Club had played with American football costumes years before and I liked the way these exoskeletons distorted their bodies and how padding inserted into pockets in the trousers emphasised muscle, creating a stylised caricature of male physique.

The hipster breeches with their laced-up crotch also added to this stereotypical masculinity and didn't lose any of their effect when adapted for girls. The flame design from Hot Rod boy racer culture was spray-painted on the armour and knitted into skullcap beanies paired with red Adidas tracksuit bottoms for three of the flag-bearers for 'Your Disco Needs You'. Originally we had used US football helmets but had ordered the wrong sizes and they looked so ridiculous that when Kylie put her size three Manolo Blahniked foot down we dropped them.

Following the success of her version of 'Dancing Queen' on the last tour, Steve and I had wanted to begin this section with another camp classic. This time it was *Flashdance*'s turn, complete with a ballet-style solo from Milena Mancini, one of our eight Italian dancers. During one of our 'friends and family' performances at Bray rehearsal studios, however, it went down like the proverbial lead balloon and was swiftly dropped.

By the end of the medley, after dancing for twenty minutes in these huge contraptions, the dancers were all on the verge of collapse so we replaced them with Dennis the Menace striped rugby shirts with 'KM' on the back for the boys, and red PVC bras from a Soho sex shop for the girls. These were paired Village People-style with flags from various countries around the world, used first as sarongs then ripped off to wave about as a tongue-in-cheek nod to the happy idea of unity of nations through disco.

POLES

CHANDELIER / DOLMITE

KYLIE   Broadway Swing   ©08-01-01 Perry Scenic Ltd

lights on the stairs etc.   curtains could be
                                     rachel

Steps had just covered 'Better The Devil You Know' (or so we were told – it sounded exactly the same to us so we will have to take their word for it). The decision was made to reinvent the song for the new Kylie audience, as we feared that the usurpers' version would be seen as the original to many of the post 'Spinning Around' fans.

As the deco skyscraper sets from old Fred Astaire routines were a key influence for the design of this section, which featured a fake black grand piano rising from beneath the stage, it seemed appropriate to reinvent the song as a forties swing number.

Oh, to dance with Fred Astaire....

Since *42nd Street* had closed its doors in the West End years before, only acts like Tap Dogs and Hot Shoe Shuffle had attempted to rejuvenate this complex and intricate dance form for a contemporary audience. As a consequence, tap had been perceived as rather old-fashioned.

The new tap arrangement of 'Devil' was introduced with a snatch of the torch song version of 'I Should Be So Lucky' from Intimate and Live. The dancers, many of whom had never tapped before, managed to carry it off dressed in the traditional top hat and tails, with canes and feather fans to detract attention from often out-of-time feet. The piano was difficult to manoeuvre and the stagehands were all bent double trying to fix it into position. Instead of the beautiful real instrument that it was supposed to be, it was one night revealed to be a hollow shell, the stagehands having placed it in the wrong position.

Kylie opened the club section with 'Physical'. This song was to have been on Baz Luhrmann's *Moulin Rouge* soundtrack album, but didn't make it to the final release as it wasn't finished in time. Steve was pleased with our results, a sexually charged grind of a song with Kylie's delivery so breathy she sounded as if she was on the brink of heart failure. Choreographer Luca Tommasini devised a five-pronged contraption to accommodate a pole-dancing routine that began with four barely decent girls piled up on its roof. The apparatus was so huge we could never properly conceal it in the wings and the girls were already so sweaty they kept sliding down the poles before it had even been wheeled on. Their Agent Provocateur stripper knickers also proved problematic as by the time they had slid down to the podium base their golden glitter fringes were stuck all over their bellies and thighs, giving the appearance of overgrown pubic wigs. Luca and I both wanted pasties (not the Cornish kind) or tit tassels as they are more commonly known, but it was impossible to stick them on between the songs, so we sewed tit tassels onto bras instead. Every night as the contraption was wheeled on, the band would have to make a concerted effort not to lose their place and the plot, so entranced were they as the girls' knickers disappeared further and further into their cute little Italian bottoms.

Kylie took to her filthy pole-dancing routine like a duck to water and was constantly coming off stage with a worried look during the quick change. 'Was that too much? Was that OK?' Naturally she toned it down the night that Ron, her dad, came to see the show. All she managed then was one of her trademark bum wiggles. Otherwise her pole-dance became filthier and filthier each night.

The strip-club set featured fake flame-throwing machines, four of them positioned across the back of the set, theoretically giving the appearance of slow-burning torches. These machines were brought in as a secondary thought. Originally I had wanted real flames blazing out but of course I hadn't realised that in theatres this was a fire risk, nor that no pyrotechnic can sustain a high flame for five minutes. The most they could manage within the safety requirements of our venues was a five-second burst.

This threw me into one of my stinking moods as I was convinced that these rules had been invented solely to wind me up. Our substitutes consisted of about four metres of pale silk chiffon propelled upwards by fans built into their base. Every night one or more would get stuck in the fans and there wasn't a single show when all four of them worked. When they did work they just resembled huge condoms flailing around and when the show went to arenas in Australia we dropped them and real pyro flame-bursts graced the stage instead.

If 'Physical' was intended as something for the boys, 'Butterfly' was for a different kind of boy and for the girls. My then flatmate Wayne Shires, a London club promoter, was behind such trendy early nineties hangouts as Bar Industria and Sex, the Friday nighter at Café de Paris. He had recently bought a club space underneath the railway arches in Vauxhall very near the famous gay cabaret pub, the Vauxhall Tavern, which hosted to many gay cabaret stars who have since clawed their way into the mainstream. Lily Savage and Julian Clary have both graced the tavern's tiny stage. Wayne's latest project Crash is a hedonistic sweatpit of a club and its reputation as one of the best gay clubs around had already reached Miami, New York, Sydney and Cape Town. The dance-floors and dim backrooms of Crash were the inspiration for the last section of On A Night Like This.

'Butterfly' was the stand-out song on the *Light Years* album. Written by Kylie, Steve and American producer Mark Pichiotti, its dance beat and harder edge were to inspire the more mature dance-orientated songs on Parlophone's *Fever* album. 'Butterfly' was quickly turned into a white label remix, with the cover stamped only with a rather *Silence of the Lambs*-style butterfly logo, and it was a success as an anonymous dance track in clubs on both sides of the Atlantic.

For the show Steve arranged an exotic, pumping intro to buy time for yet another quick change. The lighting was club-based, all high contrast golden glows and strobes giving the leather-clad muscle boys a sinister edge. Wearing black leather tracksuit bottoms, woven leather visors and hoods all designed by Fiona Doran, who later designed Kylie's white catsuit for 'Can't Get You Out Of My Head', the costumes were quickly christened by the crew 'The Gimps'. With hoods up the boys did bear a resemblance to executioners or the Grim Reaper, but the stark sexuality of the look, compared to the rest of the show's light-hearted costumes, was right for the hard tribal beats of the soundtrack. Kylie and Steve, along with half the crew, turned pale when the boys came on the first time. It was brought up at a meeting afterwards as being too extreme and possibly frightening to the 'littlies', as Kylie calls her younger audience. I changed the subject to moan about the flying johnnies during 'Physical'. One of the muscle boys' visor refused to stay on due to him sweating profusely under the low lights. Every night as Paolo flung his head around the visor flew off and he would stomp off stage cursing in Italian as I threatened to bolt it to his pretty head.

The girls were very provocative, writhing onto the stage as if they were the hounds of Lucifer himself. Their golden merkins having been given a good brush and often a trim between songs, they looked - just as had been intended - like Conan the Barbarian's handmaidens, with their woven leather strip tops again by Fiona Doran. Those

Italian girls, no matter how much grooming and powder you gave them, always danced so hard and with such passion that by the second song, when their grass skirts dropped to reveal tasselled Chloé bikinis, they all looked as if they had been dragged through a hedge backwards or flung around a bedroom for a good hour or two. Boys apparently loved this.

This post-coital chic was perfect in 'Butterfly' as they made their way onto the runway to do a very exotic and brilliant routine with five-metre-long ribbons on sticks. On the last show in Sydney the crew cut their ribbons so when the girls went to pick them up all they were left with were thin white sticks with just stubs of gold. They had little choice but to proceed to wave their ridiculous appendages around like demented conductors with some invisible orchestra, looking slightly more confused than usual. Kylie was not amused.

There was more than just a hint of nymphomania to the dancers' performance. A group scene at the beginning of the final number in the show, 'Shocked', descended into something of an orgy - Kylie would often come to the quick change with tales of the girls licking her arms and biting her legs. Some of the boys were too busy with their sweaty little hands down their own trousers and poor Sean, the tour manager, had to tell them to calm it down. The feisty Italians that Luca had cast were an amazing bunch of dancers. The power and sheer sexuality of all of them was a constant source of entertainment. It was good to see two of the boys again a year later, scantily dressed as Roman centurion 'extras' at Dolce & Gabbana's end-of-tour extravaganza in Milan for the Fever tour. The girls were christened dancing lesbos by the *Sunday Sport* as they were last seen dressed in nothing but black gaffer tape molesting Geri Halliwell at Party in the Park.

DIFFERENT NEON COLOURS - RED-ET
BLUE
PINK
ORANGE

NEON N8E SMOKE.

Encore - Space Odyssey   ©08-01-01 Perry Scenic Ltd

RAMP HIGHER THAN STAGE

The show's encore featured another set - the docking port of a space station. As it was an encore it was another chance for an entrance. The spaceship port, again a painted gauze, was circular and probably the most successful of the three designs based on *Star Wars*' Death Star and the ship from Kubrick's *2001*. Panels of the backdrop curtain were cut out and covered with masked filmy fabric, allowing lights to shine through and thus make it more three-dimensional.

A fragile scaffold was wheeled into place behind the backdrop with a small platform on the top the same height as the 'airlock' door through which Kylie would be revealed. Every night Kylie went clambering up in her Manolos, often with Leanne, her PA, trailing behind, trying to stuff the wires from her ear monitors into her costume as the quick change contingent and Phil Murphy, the Scouse stage manager, held on to the ladder, trying to keep it as steady as possible. Strobes were placed on the audience-facing side of the set and chased magnificently during the countdown introduction of the song, and a three-stepped stairway leading from the scaffold onto the back runway was put into place. Every night as the countdown reached 'three... two... one', Toby Pitts, a stalwart of our intrepid crew, would rip away the fabric panel to reveal a corseted Kylie in a backlit vortex.

She would then nervously step forward and begin to sing. The reveal never quite worked to plan and the ripping off of the door was more *Spinal Tap* than *Star Trek*. The idea was that it would slide gracefully upwards, teasing the audience first with Kylie's feet, then her legs, body and finally her head - all in silhouette.

After much moaning at post-show meetings I demanded an electronic door that would work in the correct sci-fi mode. When the costing for this simple piece of machinery came in at £5,000, Kylie had a fit and set Toby - who doubled up as a carpenter - to work. He and production manager Steve Martin came up with the ingenious solution that basically consisted of a piece of MDF, some rope, a weight and a lick of paint, and the desired effect was achieved perfectly.

As befitted a show that had more than a hint of Las Vegas, Kylie's wardrobe was designed by Julien Macdonald, a young Welsh designer who was originally celebrated for his slinky knitwear. His collections shimmered and shone under runway lights. He simply adores glamour, fame and powerful women. His shows often featured supermodels when some of his rivals thought that breed and what they represented had become passé as they pursued the nouveau drab. His creations were consistently spectacular and sexy, adorned with anything that reflected light and sparkle, from sequins through to crystals or diamonds, often paired up with luxurious furs in a way rarely seen since the happy days of eighties excess. Not for him the hideous, unflattering frumpiness that three years at St Martin's seemed to encourage. Julien celebrated the diva, the decadent archetype of the star - and women loved wearing his clothes.

In many ways Julien is Kylie's fashion counterpart and, like Kylie, in his work he sometimes risks accusations of being light and insubstantial. He is an entertainer, though his shows are not the visual operatics that Alexander McQueen favours and excels at. Julien understands the importance of celebrity and press, that the tabloid circulation is a lot higher than hip, glossy magazines like *Dazed & Confused*. He built his business on the recognition of this and his clothes get a lot of mentions in tabloid stories or gossip magazines. His creations, so brilliant with crystals, so festooned with sequins, come to life like firework displays under the flashbulbs of paparazzi.

Julien appealed to the magpie in Kylie who loved how he cut as well as the sparkle. He brought out the Ann-Margret in her. Each time she wore one of his creations she appeared on the front page of national papers. She borrowed a gold-fringed number for the launch of her book *Kylie: Evidence* and was only mildly irritated when she spotted Joely Richardson in the same dress, with the same alterations she had made, a few months later.

There was also a black jersey dress, ruched into a side gather and decorated by Julien's trademark bedazzles that she wore to the [?] music awards. A more [?] entail that night when the ever-charming Liam Gallagher branded Robbie Williams a faggot and heckled Kylie a lesbian.

Julien's most famous creation for Kylie was the asymmetric silver dress she wore for her MTV awards performance with Robbie and for her guest appearance at his Manchester concert. Robbie totally lost the plot and came out in more than a little sweat, as Kylie oozed her way from behind the band and was almost catapulted into the air, scissorlift reveal like a human cannon ball before delivering one of her most confident performances as she bumped and grinded her way through a rendition of 'Kids' that stole the show. She wore a grey version of this dress for 'Physical'.

[We] trundled along one [evening] turning a couple of months before the tour to Julien's studio in disused Notting Hill theatre. An assistant who had the mind-numbing task of sewing all of the beloved 'cryst-als' - as he pronounced it with his soft Welsh lilt - on to his creations, was dispatched to the coffee shop as we weren't making much sense in our caffeine-deprived state. Naturally we had left everything to the last minute and hadn't realised the time it took to bedazzle a size eight dress in crystals. We sent the poor studio hands into overtime overdrive, diligently beading away as if their lives depended upon it. Some would show up for fittings weeks later, staggering around cross-eyed and pallid, shadows of their former selves, fingers sore and covered with glitter.

Julien would arrive at a fitting and Kylie would announce that she wanted more sparkles, sending them all scurrying back to the studio, scouring the carpets for any lost, forgotten crystals. The whole operation bore a similarity to the mice on the mouse organ from TV's *Bagpuss*. Kylie's top for the 'Love Boat' number was so heavily encrusted that it stood up by itself and totally flattened her chest. It was so scratchy from the dried glue that held the crystals in place that it brought her out in a rash so it was continually redesigned until we finally settled on a pink-striped [?] with a [?] splattering of [crystals]. [?] with this Julien created a [?] beaded mini skirt, the waistband crammed with silver [?] of differing sizes. The [?] itself was Tiffany blue with pink stripes and similarly covered with tiny bugle-bead tassels that were so fragile they invariably came off, scattering thousands of tiny beads across the stage every night.

For her entrance on the anchor we used the design for the split-sleeved dressing gown that Kylie had worn in the video for 'Please Stay'. Very Abba, and very seventies Playboy, [?] version of this was given the Macdonald touch, it disappeared looking like a nightie for an inmate of the [?] Clinic but returned enraptured by a couturier with huge tropical flowers and leaves which Julien then proceeded to cover in more 'cryst-als'.

[For her [?] medley] he designed a skin-tight red leather ensemble based on a seventies denim design, with a big door knocker of a belt buckle, diamond buttons, and flame bell-bottoms. The outfit was accessorised with a Stephen Jones red leather cap with a huge gold chain across the front and an extended asymmetric peak. Kylie thought she looked like a bus conductor and wasted no time in ditching it after painstakingly picking off the chain and chucking it into her bottomless handbag where it lives to this day, often making guest appearances at photo shoots when a touch of last-minute customising is called for.

Every night Kylie would put herself through twenty minutes of vigorous dancing in this leather ensemble and slump into the quick change with the outfit literally stuck to her, apparently about to pass out as we peeled away the red leather to get her into her next outfit. As the tour dates went on and on and on, out of sheer boredom and with little else to do, I decided to replace the shirt with a little red leather biker jacket which I had deluded myself into thinking was more eighties and therefore more appropriate.

A middle-aged queen with a handlebar moustache from an Oxford Street leather store specialising in black leather chaps very kindly took the commission and delivered the jacket in two days. It didn't solve Kylie's heat exhaustion however, and she finally decided she could make do more for fashion and flung the jacket across the quick change room, demanding a T-shirt. 'A T-shirt!' I cried. 'Are you mad?' The next day in her dressing room we set about one of the tour T-shirts, trying desperately to come up with something for the evening's performance. By this time the novelty of life on the road had well and truly worn off. 'This is so Madonna,' I muttered under my breath, at which Kylie snatched up the scissors, brandished them wildly and set about me from across the room.

The angels who delivered us from this T-shirt hell were Kylie's mum Carol and her nan. They stayed up all night slaving over the sewing machine and overlocker, and came up with the solution - an asymmetric black jersey top tied in a knot on one shoulder, and customised with Kylie's nickname 'Min' along the bottom.

For the Broadway tribute, top hat and tails were the only option. In the androgynous style for which she became known, it was Marlene Dietrich who had first made the tuxedo fashionable for women in the thirties, and Madonna flirted with the look in her tour The Girlie Show and when promoting her book Sex. She crowned the look with a lopsided beret perched on her famous blonde locks.

Our cause was clearly more Midler than Madonna and, as Julien didn't 'do' tailoring at the time, ladies' bespoke tailor Pamela Blundell, formerly of Copperwheat Blundell, was called upon. She created Kylie's cream satin tuxedo suit, and Stephen Jones provided us with a mini top hat in the same fabric. The lounge brogues were the compulsory Manolo Blahniks, and Kylie squealed like an over-excited Julien at the prospect of dancing in what she called 'flats', though in fact they had a heel of about an inch.

We never really had a definite idea of what we wanted for the costumes for the club section, the results never quite worked. The diamond chain top had been created by jewellery designer Johnny Rocket as a showpiece for Julien's catwalk collection and the gold leather trousers had been run up by an eccentric Indian leather merchant known rather enigmatically as Jagger. He had a tiny studio and showroom just off London's Brick Lane that was always buried beneath piles of beer cans and was invariably always closed.

Kylie's starship captain outfit had been inspired by the lyrics of 'Light Years', in which she was the purser of a spaceship cruiser. Air hostess costumes from the sixties were researched and embellished with all kinds of cosmic kitsch elements particular to that decade's vision of the future. Eventually we settled for the colourways of some long since vanished airline and cross-referenced them with an early nineties Thierry Mugler corset. The result was a baby blue corset dress with an added white front panel that we were forced to extend due to the continual guest appearance of la Minogue's perky breasts. A pleated netball skirt in the same fabric finished the outfit. Stephen Jones created a miniature teardrop-shaped air hostess hat in white satin with a blue plastic visor that resembled a paper plate from a distance, and the crew would all dance around in the wings in the suitably robotic style of the choreography with various pieces of crockery nicked from catering on their heads.

To end the show were the obligatory white hot pants, white vest tied in midriff - a Mothercare age twelve - and another one of Julien's Elvis-style belt buckles. This cute little ensemble was finished off with a little kerchief, Penelope Pitstop-style.

It is difficult to say what it was about the On A Night Like This tour that left me quietly disheartened. There had been so many technical difficulties, and it seemed to go on for ever, often in the same venue for a week. Kylie and myself were bored senseless, frequently attempting to redesign the show just for something to do, whilst Terry, Kylie's manager, would run for cover.

Kylie succumbed to a debilitating bug in Melbourne but she refused to cancel. Instead a doctor had to stand by during the quick changes to give her bursts of oxygen and an anti-nausea and anti-dizziness injection into her behind. I will never forget the image of Kylie, white as a sheet and apparently on the verge of collapse as she swayed on top of that grand piano. Almost everyone backstage had a teary moment that night. Such was the genuine affection and concern she earned from her crew, but that night seemed to put a damper on the rest of the tour.

Some of the dancers got so carried away towards the end of the tour that it was sometimes difficult to know who to fret over their wanting and who not. Each had become a mini celebrity and their personalities quietly became overpowering on a stage that was meant to only star a band and backing dancers. Everything seemed to distract from rather than frame the woman around whom the show was built.

There was the added factor that the very concept upon which On A Night Like This had been built was one of retrospective celebration, a reintroduction of a star to an audience whose familiarity with Kylie did not extend beyond her recent 'comeback', whereas to everybody behind the scenes no reintroduction had ever been neccessary. Kylie had never been away.

A new direction was called for. Camp Kylie closed its doors for refurbishment.

10

:

La la
la

Miles Leonard and Jamie Nelson, Parlophone's A&R, called Kylie, Terry and myself for a meeting in early January 2001 to reassess the year that had witnessed Kylie's return to the pop charts. They were particulary excited that morning, having received a demo from former Mud star Rob Davis, and Cathy Dennis. We knew as soon as Miles played the track in his office that this was *the* song.

There had been a feeling at Parlophone that last year's campaign for the *Light Years* album had started brilliantly, but had slightly lost track. We were simply finding our feet again within the new pop marketplace. Miles, in particular, was uncomfortable with the camp elements of *Light Years*, seeing it as patronising and redundant to produce camp songs for a gay audience as Kylie's audience was broadening rapidly. He wanted to push her boundaries again, feeling that he and Parlophone had to make the A&R direction produce something more contemporary. They had signed her to develop her music, not keep it where it was.

No one had been too impressed with the fourth and final English single from *Light Years*, 'Please Stay'. Fans campaigned against the track's release, favouring the obvious camp 'Your Disco Needs You'. Miles felt that to release that track would be to push Kylie deeper into a box she already occupied and feared that if they pursued that line she would find it harder than ever to climb out.

'Please Stay' is similar to Kylie's early work from her PWL canon – polished but vacuous, unlike her millennium comeback album. Placed after 'Spinning Around' and 'Kids', the song's release revealed little development or direction: one step forward, then one step back. With the *Dukes of Hazzard*-style backroom bar homage of a video, complete with fireman's pole pool table routine, we had little choice but to camp it up, but we also did want to try and hold onto the sexy edge that we had been pushing with Kylie's flirtatious style and the more overt raunchiness of our girl dancers. The girls pranced around the pool table in Luella Bartley knickers with ribbons cascading from the sides and a range of daywear tops from Agent Provocateur, amongst other places.

The two boys appeared in tight jeans and western shirts, their crotches padded for that *Dukes of Hazzard* bulge that had kept me entertained all those years ago. Kylie wore an Abba-style dressing gown that, as if by magic, changed colour from gold to red as she slid down the pole. The video was a camp barn dance. Parlophone had nearly choked their croissants during one of their weekly Monday morning label meetings, as they watched a recording of the single performed in front of Prince Charles in the Royal Variety Performance the previous December, when we interpreted the song as a Moulin Rouge/can-can number with Kylie dressed as a scarlet courtesan in the Victorian attire of the music halls.

The organisation of the performance had also been a nightmare due to Juicy Lucy on one of her nights out at some salubrious Camden drinking emporium, taking a drunken fall in her Westwood stilettos, snapping her heel and her arm in the process. She was more upset about the former, but I was left with no help and with a huge number of people to style. That was when we met Leanne, a friend of a friend who became the saviour of the day as she was promptly dispatched to the BBC's costume hire warehouse to unearth vintage can-can dresses from period productions. She was so efficient in her task that Kylie promptly nicked her to assist her, and I was left assistant-less again while Juicy

recovered. The variety performance was all a bit much for poor Leanne who was left waiting in the rain for a taxi with rails and rails of clothes and with only the slow warmth of a Vacuum for company, all of us having 'done one' after the show. I think she was relieved to have escaped my histrionics and employment.

However, the burlesque elements of the revue-style number hit Kylie's record company hard, even though sales of *Light Years* soared the following week. When 'Please Stay' didn't fare as well as its predecessors Parlophone realised it was time to take stock.

'Can't Get You Out Of My Head' took its inspiration from eighties electro, encompassing a fresh interpretation of the dance track, knowingly and ironically produced. With its nod to the past, sharp and minimal, metronomic beats and naive lyrical content made the song an immediate pop/dance crossover, the production enabling it to be played in its naked and purest form without the customary prerequisite remix (of which there have been many). From the school of Moroder and slightly more polished than the raw electronica and Teutonic beats of Kraftwerk, it was digital music at its most mesmerising. Its deep bass rhythms pound through the speakers as hypnotically as a religious chant. The naive lyric 'la, la, la' is tirelessly repeated, creating a sublime pop mantra for the twenty-first century. The lyrics are ambiguous, both disposable and disturbing, hinting at obsession and the desire to actually get some haunting notion out of one's head.

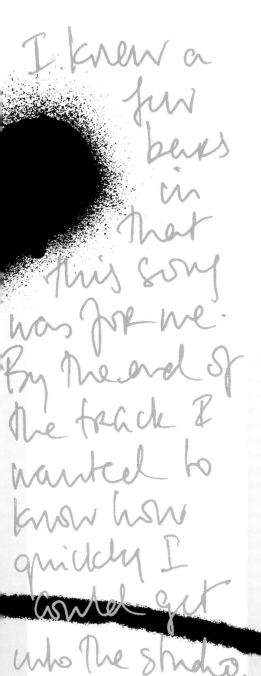

I knew a few bars in that this song was for me. By the end of the track I wanted to know how quickly I could get into the studio. Though I had already started writing for what was to become 'Fever', this gave us a benchmark & defined what we were hoping to achieve with the album in a way that words could not.

Everything fell into place upon hearing the song for the first time, even though six months passed before release. Its style and feel suggested a new creative direction that was to be slick, minimalist and postmodern. This journey was most acutely expressed in the KylieFever2002 tour. For now, the song was a revelatory moment and a whole plethora of visual ideas flowed simply from the music.

Often, on previous occasions, we had applied what we wanted to do over the top of the track, manipulating style to sound; it wasn't common for the inspiration to actually flow naturally from a piece of music. Almost architecturally spare in its design and production, the song and subsequent album gave birth to a much tighter vision, a stripping down of complex cluttering, leaving Kylie framed simply and effectively.

The imagery for the *Fever* album and subsequent tour was an exercise in contemporary pop iconography. I was inspired by Jean-Paul Goude's photographs of Grace Jones in his book *Jungle Fever*, and by Grace's groundbreaking one-woman show, itself a celebration of the power of the female performer. Grace perfected a cocktail of danger, power, sex and raw instinct, ingredients which were always evident in photographs of her. Her album covers are instantly recognisable and memorable. I was keen to endow Kylie with some of Grace's more confrontational allure. I perused vintage album covers for hours: Blondie, Roxy Music, Neneh Cherry... I was keen to create an image that would encapsulate the icon that is Kylie. I was also keen to portray her with the tools of her craft – headphones, speakers and a microphone.

Vincent Peters was again called upon to capture Kylie, trading the ocean blue of an Ibiza horizon for the white wall of a studio in Kensal Rise:

I got that microphone and at some point we tied her up with it. It is simply between her and the prop. Whatever you do with a picture, it will always be a metaphor. You could run a rabbit over on a road and photograph it, it will be interpreted as a metaphor. That is what a photograph is, it symbolises different things. The fact with Kylie is that Kylie herself and her body language pulls enough metaphors, enough associations, that you don't have to put anything else in there.

The silhouette on the cover features Kylie holding a microphone to her lips, linking her inextricably to her profession. She is both posed and singing, the two key ingredients in the Kylie mix.

Puff Daddy was also having his picture taken that day in the studio upstairs, surrounded by his usual entourage of about ten burly minders. As Vincent took Kylie outside in the rain to soak her through for a wet T-shirt look, poor Mr Coombs was left on his own as all the minders' mobiles started ringing at once and his posse rushed outside for a better reception and a better view of Kylie's nipples as her dress became see-through.

The album and artwork were designed by graphic bod Tony Hung, a new member of the Kylie team, who created a minimal, electronic jagged logo and developed a tag 'K' logo that inspired the subsequent stage design of the show. The tag was a 'stamp' confirming that she had now become an immediately recognisable brand.

Dawn Shadforth was asked to direct the video for 'Can't Get You Out Of My Head'. I had worked with Dawn since 'Spinning Around' – a couple of months previously for a video for a track called 'Living In A Magazine' by Zoot Woman – and it was good to be together yet again. The Zoot video was a satire on modern-day fashion and the DIY approach of many young designers. Customising had become something of a trend, and we customised everything in sight making a whole series of dresses out of bin liners, spray paint and plastic knives and forks, a comment on how fashion had become almost a parody of itself in its search for conceptual innovation. Zoot Woman already had a regular designer, and that is how Fiona Doran, who had a label called Mrs Jones, came to work with Kylie.

We had used Fee's designs for the photo shoot for the On A Night Like This tour brochure, shot by young Spanish photographer Xevi. One of the dresses was a red draped and hooded jersey affair, the hood becoming one of Fee's signatures. Fee is a consummate craftswoman, possessing the skill to transform her ideas into living garments that actually work. She specialises in intricate leather work, threading, weaving and crocheting thin leather strips into the most beautiful forms, as displayed in a dress inspired by a 'butcher's curtain' for 'In Your Eyes'. Cutting-edge, raw and new, her designs are often inspired by music. She professes to be 'a bit of an old soulgirl at heart. Remember Zap and Computer Love, Grandmaster Flash...?' Fee has a unique approach to her work, with female musical icons Grace Jones and Blondie cited as two major inspirations. Her dual love of fashion and music collide in her part-time job as a DJ. I was keen for Fee and Kylie to meet.

Kylie and I went to Fee's house in Kensal Green where, hanging up, was what appeared to be a huge shroud. Kylie tried the six-foot-long outfit on with a pair of Fee's size eight heels. The hood added to the length of the silhouette and the side splits on the legs were the result of Kylie saying 'higher... higher...' as Fee attacked the jersey with her scissors.

Fee's love of all things hooded derived from a dress that she had bought years ago from a charity shop:

As I put the hood up I felt like someone else. It immediately gives you a power. It's like wearing a hat... you can hide behind it a little bit. It has the whole Virgin Mary thing as well. I remember when I was on a beach full of topless women and I had my bikini on and I kept getting chatted up. There were all these girls with their big boobs just hanging out... It is intrigue that is sexy, just seeing glimpses rather than the whole.

The white hooded slashed-to-the-waist-jumpsuit she made for the video of 'Can't Get You Out Of My Head' is her most famous design.

In the video Kylie becomes the sexy urban Madonna. All white to signify purity, Kylie's costume once again provides a provocative modesty as she looms towards the camera and thus the viewer, her lips red, full and pouting. Her spectacular dance titillates, but at the same time deters, as she lures the viewer into her seduction and then aggressively repels with a sudden choreographed jerk. Kylie is separated from her dancers by the contrasting colour of her outfit, but also by her almost holy, untouchable and perfect beauty. There are elements of the goddess about her again, crowned with an immaculate aura of light or halo.

But then Kylie taps into a pagan psyche with powerful and loaded imagery combined with the chanting chorus. This modern Venus conveys modesty and mystery, but she is not submissive, as in many classically reclining or coy poses. On the contrary, she is authoritative and commanding.

In tradition the dance of the seven veils symbolises an uncovering and a revelation, an ancient version of the striptease and the pole-dance. It is a dance that empowers and seduces. Andy Warhol said, 'With everything changing so fast, you don't have a chance of finding your fantasy image intact by the time you are ready for it.' Kylie fills that niche perfectly. She is where fantasy and clothes meet.

'Can't Get You Out Of My Head' was the beginning of a visual journey that encapsulated the combination of performance, technology and artistry centred around Kylie. It was to continue throughout the imagery of the *Fever* album. The video became one of the most played of recent years, a highly visual fragment of pop entertainment. It reflected the song's technological reliance and simplicity whilst also retaining elements of early eighties pop videos such as Visage's 'Fade to Grey'. The bleached-out face of heavily painted Steve Strange, leaving sensuous lips and mesmeric eyes, gave the video a touch of modernised and perfected glamour similar to Kylie's. The idea of the veil also appeared in 'Fade to Grey' as Princess Julia cavorted in her interpretation of the dance of the seven veils, wearing a bed sheet on her head. Kylie's make-up, by Karen Alder, was influenced by the airbrushed make-up of the early eighties, inherited from Warhol's legacy of silk-screened celebrity portraits depicting white faces with vividly coloured lips and eyes.

Kylie had three other looks for the video: a black *Star Trek*-inspired dress accessorised with Vivienne Westwood driving gloves, a white leather tracksuit, again courtesy of Fiona, with Gucci white bra and the Gucci lilac ribbon square dress for the roof-top scene. This dress was actually a copy, the Gucci press sample being far too big for Kylie. She wore it with black knee-length boots - actually sprayed white ones which needed respraying between each take as half the paint came off on her legs as she danced. The choreography was by innovative American Michael Rooney, who produced an uncontrived routine based on robotics. It was at once contemporary, quirky and visually eccentric.

I had been eager to separate Kylie from the hordes of other artists who appear on Saturday morning pop shows with the same old dancers in the same old outfits. For an artist whose roots firmly lay on the dance-floor, I found it strange that she had never been associated with groundbreaking dance routines beyond the ass slapping in 'Spinning Around', when she could obviously dance. I was keen for her to develop a style of dance unique to her, in the same way that Madonna had pilfered Vogueing, for example. I had always been mesmerised by dancing and dancers, their skill, co-ordination and discipline seeming so alien and magical to me with my two size eleven left feet.

The electronic beats of the music on 'Can't Get You Out Of My Head' lean naturally to a form of robotic-style movement which we had explored briefly for 'Light Years' on the previous tour but we felt that we hadn't pushed this far enough. Michael Rooney's choreography was fantastic, both avant-garde and accessible - wherever Kylie goes she is confronted by little kids performing this dance routine. 'Can't Get You Out Of My Head' and its retro-futurist sound enabled me to pursue my secret life as a closet sci-fi nerd.

I had always been a huge fan of TV sci-fi, particularly *Doctor Who*. A timelord with twelve lives, The Doctor possessed the power of regeneration, maintaining the essence of character through revolutions of visual identity. The changing faces and different incarnations of his mutating form may fancifully be said to parallel Kylie's own career. Even the eighties version of the TV show's synthesised theme produced by the BBC's Radiophonic Workshop with its 'dum de dum' electronic bass line bore a similarity to the moog-like beats of 'Can't Get You Out Of My Head'.

We had assembled a team of fantastic classically trained dancers, many from theatre backgrounds rather than from the humdrum denim world of commercial dance. I had noticed Alec Mann on stage in the West End in the production of *Notre Dame de Paris*, which starred Kylie's sister Dannii. I had gone to the show with Kylie's mum, Carol. We had gone back to see the show four times, and every time I thought that Alec's chiselled features and sharp precision of movement were perfect for the look I wanted, and so he enrolled into our mad, mad world as Kylie's dance partner. Tim Noble, who had performed for years in *Starlight Express,* originally came to our attention as one of the roller-skaters for 'Spinning Around'. He became dance captain on the tour.

When it came to booking the dancers for the tour, I was quick to book Mancunian acrobat Terry 'tumble tot' Kvasnik, whom I had also spotted in *Notre Dame*. Dancers Rod Buchanan, Pia Driver and Melanie Teal also came from the same musical, so for many the tour was a bit of a luvvie reunion. The remaining dancers were all auditioned specifically, most of them coming from the world of contemporary dance.

It was vital for Kylie and me to have a team of dancers that we could trust and who looked sufficiently different from their contemporaries. I needed to know that they took the job seriously as dancers, that they took pride in their precision of movement instead of trying to steal the attention at every available opportunity from the star herself.

We had wanted all the dancers to wear the same thing in the video, part of our desire to create a backdrop of android drones. The anonymity of these dancers meant that nothing could detract from the centralised power of Kylie. As a tribute to Kraftwerk, the boys were dressed in the band's trademark red shirts and black ties, their faces covered with a Rudi Gernrich-inspired perspex visor to give them a futurist edge. Pretty boys and girls were auditioned for their androgynous looks.

The girl dancers wore red versions of Kylie's *Star Trek* uniform from her driving scene, with flat black thigh boots that came from a basement in Camden for twenty quid a pair. Their outfits were finished with a red perspex cone, a feminine take on the boys' red 'data shields', giving them tunnel vision and focus as well as bestowing on them an immediate other-worldliness. As the styling process reached its culmination, the dancers were becoming appropriately dehumanised. The white costumes were based on *Star Wars* stormtroopers' hooded white jumpsuits, with black panel detailing, all made by Stevie Stewart.

Stevie and her partner David 'Lola' Holah created the Bodymap label in the eighties. She remembers Kylie buying from the Bodymap boutique in Hyper Hyper years ago on Kensington High Sreet. Bodymap was a fashion concept and company that created fusions of bold prints on innovative modern fabrics, combining Stevie and David's artistry of shape, pattern and cut with form and function that created a fluidity, an ease of movement. Bodymap's sensibility made them the perfect choice to design costumes for Michael Clarke's ballet company's theatrical productions, their clothes coming to life in the incredible avant-garde movement that made Clarke the 'enfant terrible' of contemporary ballet. Stevie was introduced to me by Princess Julia, a mutual friend, when I needed a last-minute frock running up for Kylie. She was the ideal executioner when it came to creating and realising my ideas to clothe our own dance troupe. Stevie worked in a Kentish Town studio with machinist Sandy Gordon, who I had previously known from terrorising the Vivienne Westwood and Copperwheat Blundell studios when I had worked there as a stylist, earning himself a reputation as one of the best machinists in London. The pair have made many of the costumes worn by Kylie and her dancers over the last three years (including Kylie's courtesan outfit from the Royal Variety Performance), culminating with KylieFever2002.

In another scene of the video, the girls wore mini netball skirts that we had hacked in half, string vests which we had also cut to shreds with two elbow patches sewn on to cover breasts. Their blonde white bowl wigs made them look like the killer kids from *Village of the Damned*. We built our own version of a clone army. The designs of their costumes were both bold and graphic and perfectly complemented Dawn's post-production created utopias.

The dehumanising of the dancers and the choreography were driving forces integral to the imagery in Kylie's next two videos, 'In Your Eyes' and 'Love At First Sight', the latter a veritable carnival of kookiness. For 'In Your Eyes', Kylie and I had by now become slightly obsessed with body popping and a street interpretation of robotic, jerky movement, and with a core of dancers now assembled we could pursue this to a fuller extent. Their costumes reflected this mix of hip hop chic with sci-fi lunacy, old school Adidas and Airtex tracksuits with legs and arms cut off to reveal 'mechanical' knee pads underneath, combining man and machine. The girls looked like aliens in their lace bodysuits. 'Love At First Sight' featured a race of yellow robomen and a cyberdelic ballet troop, a dehumanised mirror to the human element present in the form of Kylie.

While his called me childest, for watched
'The Simpsons'. He said this with his
nose buried in a 'DOCTOR WHO' FANZINE!!

Michael Rooney, unfortunately for us, lived in LA, so it was difficult to establish a continuous working relationship. I now had a forthcoming tour to choreograph. I knew what it was I was looking for, but lack of choreographic jargon meant that I found it hard to express it in words. We had worked with various choreographers, all remarkable in their own way but failing to give a pop routine the depth and integrity that we desired.

The answer to my prayers came in the form of movement junkie Rafael Bonachela. I attended a show by England's leading contemporary dance company, Ballet Rambert, and couldn't believe my eyes as I watched, awestruck, a work of Rafael's called 'Linear Remains'. There was no discernible music, just ambient techno sound. Movement for movement's sake, it was a work of pure genius. Rafael explains it as follows:

The movement I create is very particular to me. I try to create my own physical language. It is movement in a pure form. I play with the body, I modify it, I strangle it, I lengthen it and I try and get it to move differently. I like my dancers to look beautiful and dangerous, extreme.

His first piece for us was a performance on the Brit Awards. It was an experiment to see if he could translate his work into a pop arena, a trial run for the tour.

The man/machine hybrid we'd been experimenting with was pushed to its limits when we created the Kyborgs for the performance piece which opened the ceremony. Based on a faceless, lithe robot which had featured in a *Doctor Who* episode, jeweller Johnny Rocket and I created a whole race of robotic drones. Johnny created a 'helmet' that completely covered the face, based upon my drawings which consisted of elements of Marvel superhero Silver Surfer, *Star Trek*'s Borg character Seven of Nine and a cyclist's helmet. The helmets were metallic silver and under the light they took the form of liquid mercury, distorting the shape of the head. The sculpted silver bodysuits, made again by Stevie Stewart and Sandy Gordon, were skin-tight, creating the perfect silhouette to display and enhance Rafael's choreography.

Some of the dancers were miffed that I was covering up their faces and denying them their three-minute fix of fame, which slightly annoyed me. If they couldn't take pleasure in movement itself and the visual effect that they were generating, then they were welcome to pack their bags and audition for Steps. Removed from a human backdrop of dancers, Minogue's clone army framed her well, and she stood out as immediately iconic as the only human form.

Raf had never even been to a pop concert prior to working with us, so it was a massive task for him to take on choreographing a two-hour show. I loved him, his ideas and his fresh interpretation of the music. To perform his work & to watch his movement & choreography take shape and form was so inspiring. Avant-garde movement in a pop context was exactly what we were hoping to find. On top of that, Raf was, without a doubt, 'one of us'

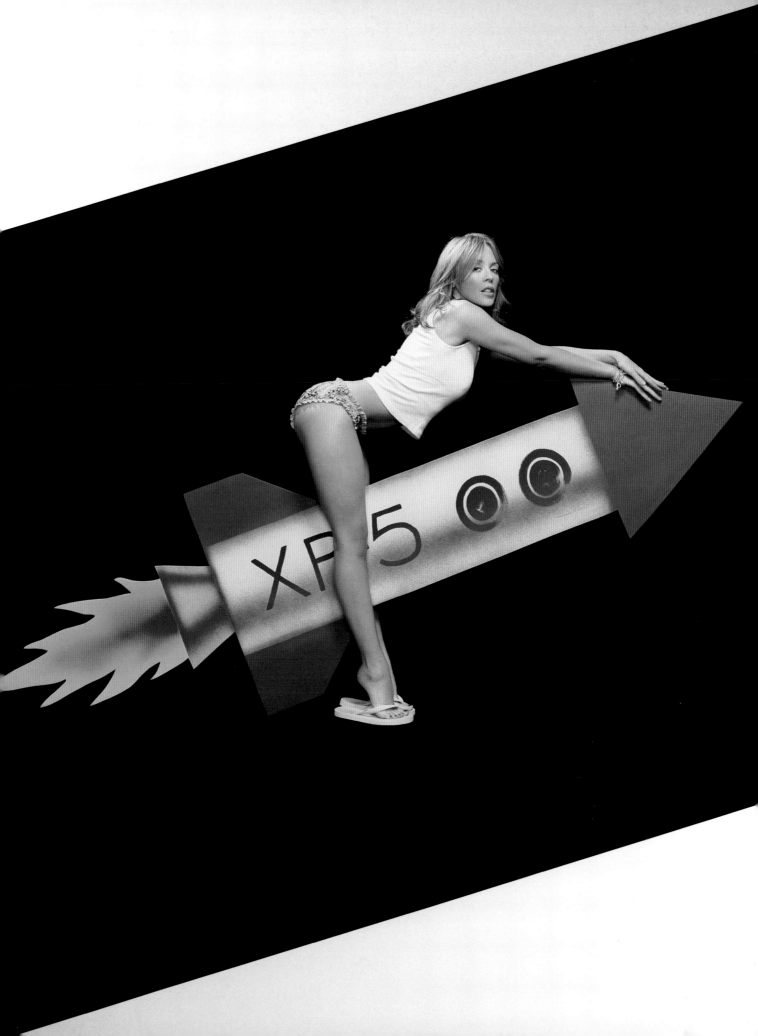

Kylie and I had begun a relationship with Dolce & Gabbana and it was they who created the white corseted dress she had worn at the Brits. The fact that we had attracted the interest of probably two of the world's most famous and distinguished designers was a sign that we were on the right track and whatever the peculiar blend of visual voodoo we were weaving, it was working. Salvo Nicosia, Dolce & Gabbana's star liaison, was and is a delight to work with and was quickly integrated within the expanding fold of Kylie's creative circle.

It's a unique experience to have a designer work with clothes while they're on you, and I've been in this situation numerous times. Whether it's Dolce and Gabbana slashing a suede and diamante coat with a giant pair of scissors, Giambatista at Ungaro tailoring the fall of a jersey dress or Julien Macdonald throwing more crystals onto an impossibly small gown, you feel like you are creating something together. There's a mutual respect and excitement about the fact that there is harmony between their designs and the way I will wear them. When I was little I used to think that 'LONDON, PARIS, MILAN' were names that featured only on that glamorous icon the perfume bottle, not on my itinerary.

With the *Fever* album going straight to Number Three in the Billboard charts in the States, Kylie was now a huge international star. As the stakes became higher, suddenly the whole world was watching. The pressure was on to pull off an amazing and memorable tour.

I had to keep telling myself, 'You're not given more than you can handle.' In the space of about two months everything had changed. Though I had been accustomed to a certain level of attention for many years, this shift in gear took me completely by surprise. Suddenly I had even more demands on my time, and on myself. I had to, and still am, trying to find the balance. I feel like I'm surfing this almighty wave and I know how hard I've paddled to get there. It's awesome, it's exciting and I also know it could come crashing down upon me. You don't take a risk if you're unaware of any danger.

Alan Macdonald had been a close friend of mine for some time. Every morning we had coffee at Bar Italia on Soho's Frith Street. We would watch the world go by and compare and contrast our co-dependent existences, two grumpy old gits like Soho's answer to *The Muppets'* Statler and Waldorf. Fags rampant and caps on heads, we sat there, often for hours, simply procrastinating, harassing Dini the waiter who makes the best coffee in London or bitching about the passing sights of Old Compton Street.

Alan is a world-class procrastinator. A man with a wealth of creative experience, with a honed aesthetic eye, he speaks with a cool authority, and has an exceptional perception of things. A constant companion and friend, his inspiration has been felt through much of my work for as long as I have known him. He is just one of those people who inspires, somebody who loves to teach and loves to learn as he's also a keen student of humanity. He has worked in virtually every creative field: in fashion, jewellery, furniture design, art, pop videos and film. His presence in any project is enriching, bringing a unique approach, an open mind and the know-how to transform ideas into reality.

I, on the other hand, have ideas, but seldom have a clue how to translate them into reality. Alan has worked as an art director on films for years, the culmination of working for ages as a set designer and collaborator for avant-garde film maker John Maybury, whose feature film *Love is the Devil*, the story of artist Francis Bacon, is a definitive example of Alan's aesthetic approach. He has a caustic wit, greeting me every morning with, 'Hello drear.' 'Hello drearest,' I reply, 'how are you today?' 'Terrible,' is the unvarying answer.

I asked him to work on the KylieFever tour. He had been lurking behind the scenes for years and I needed his help with what was to be the biggest (and most expensive) project we had ever undertaken. The tour's creative direction was a total joint effort, me submerging Alan in a world of dancing androids, and him scribbling away for hours, making sure that whatever themes or concepts we planned to pursue and develop in the show could actually be achieved. We sat outside Bar Italia for about three months, disrupted only by therapy sessions or the increasing demands of Kylie's schedule.

The concept was to present a 'cutting-edge' music and dance performance piece inspired by the design of contemporary opera and dance rather than traditional musical theatre which was the inspiration behind On A Night Like This. We wanted the show to be a streamlined experience, a logical progression to accompany Kylie's *Fever* album featuring a stripping-down, both visually and musically, to a more precise, modern and sparse sound. This was most profoundly expressed in the design of the stage itself, which referred heavily to modern architecture and to a minimalist concept, but still allowed embellishment and transformation through lighting, video, costume and performance.

The focus was unmistakably Kylie. Her music provided the central impetus for the direction of the show. And the emphasis was strictly the Parlophone Kylie, with references to the past reworked. Alan and I were keen that the tour would showcase Kylie's personas in all their varied guises. The idea was to create a frame around Kylie, and this time the frame was minimal by design to emphasise the postmodern pop star, a Kylie defined not only by her music, but by her performance and image.

We were keen to bring a darkness to Kylie's glittering pop world. We wanted to give her frothiness weight, to submerge Kylie, who had become a definitive postmodern pop star, into a world of pop culture references and benchmarks that were as diverse as Ziggy Stardust, Andy Warhol, Eminem, *Doctor Who, A Clockwork Orange*, and the Buffalo look from Vivienne Westwood's early eighties collection, Witches, which had featured prints and knits incorporating the graffiti of New York street artist Keith Haring.

I was primarily driven by my dissatisfaction with the On A Night Like This tour. I wanted something somehow deeper in content, more stimulating visually, something more avant-garde. I needed to be challenged. I remembered seeing Madonna's Blonde Ambition tour in 1990, being held in rapture at the design of the costumes by Jean-Paul Gaultier and at the show's content, which featured a fairly political agenda of sex and Catholicism, amongst other themes, that have become synonymous with the artist that is Madonna. The visual panache of the performance and the undercurrent of an agenda had entertained, but also had inspired. Like that tour, I wanted our show to have an impact and to work on different levels, to produce something that would linger in the memory and likewise challenge its audience, while not resorting to confrontational controversy, which isn't Kylie's 'thing'.

Alan was keen to pursue a technological theme for the stage set, and as Kylie had become a video artist over the years, it seemed natural and relevant to incorporate five video screens into the set that would rise and fall, reveal and conceal, and entertain the audience during the stage transformations. The idea was to use the screens as part of the set itself, as part of the architecture that would establish an environment and mood. In 'Sex In Venice', for example, we decided that they would display an image of a chandelier and red velvet curtains which would open to reveal a sunset.

Video and film artist John Maybury supplied us with vast amounts of amazing, surreal videoscapes and imagery, the result of more than fifteen years of work. The time vortex and psychedelic maelstroms depicted in 'Cybertronica' were actually created by filming slow pans of fruit and vegetables, which were then rapidly speeded up. 'Cybertronica' also featured footage of the late, great disco terrorist-cum-performance-artist Leigh Bowery dancing away in our show to 'I Feel Love'. Leigh, like Kylie, was born near Melbourne, in a tiny little town called Sunshine. It seemed ironic to display the two extremes of suburban Australia's offspring. I hope Leigh would have been amused.

We worked on the tour for months. Joining Alan and me for meetings at Kylietowers – which had been christened 'The Drains' by Alan, due to the ever dripping, frequently overflowing drains – were tour manager Sean Fitzpatrick and Steve Anderson, both of whom wanted to push the gamut as far as they could. We spent many evenings and nights together smoking countless packets of fags, piecing together the themes and influences that we wanted to embrace.

Steve had been inspired by the soundtrack to the film *Moulin Rouge* with its prevalent philosophy of mixing something old, something borrowed, something new and something blue. He created an incredible soundtrack, featuring songs from all periods of Kylie's career, including *Impossible Princess* and 'German Bold Italic', Kylie's nutty collaboration with Towa Tei, to truly represent Kylie's musical output.

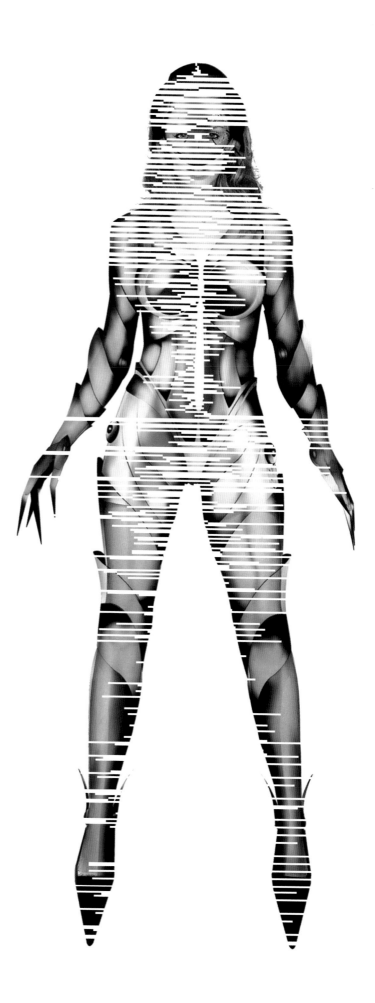

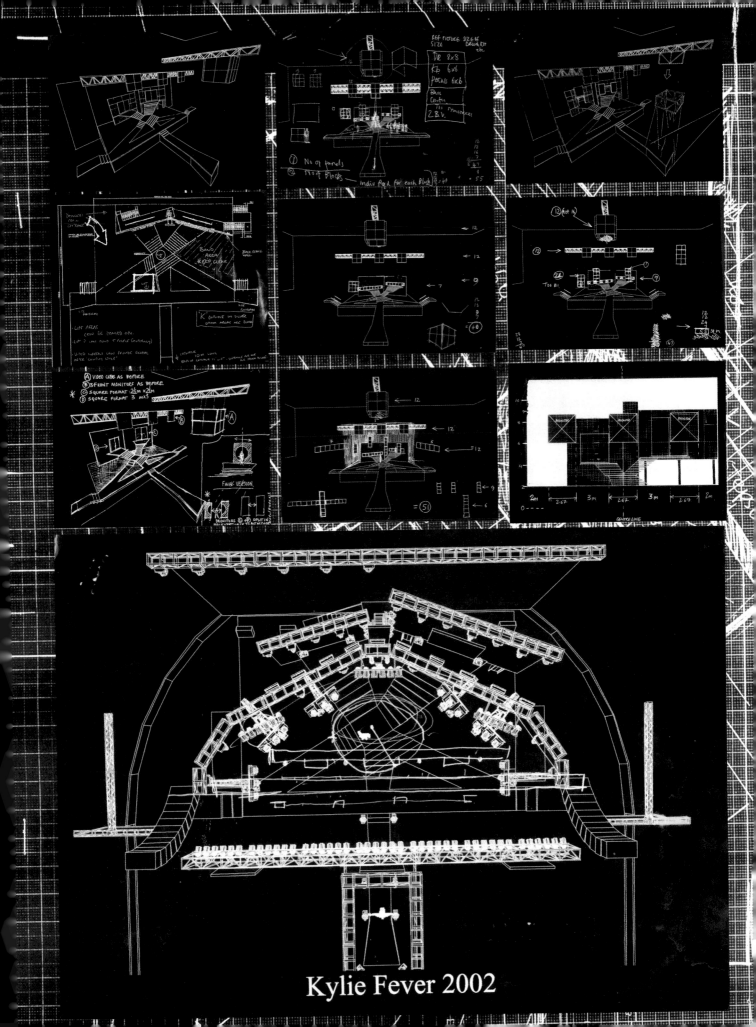

Kylie Fever 2002

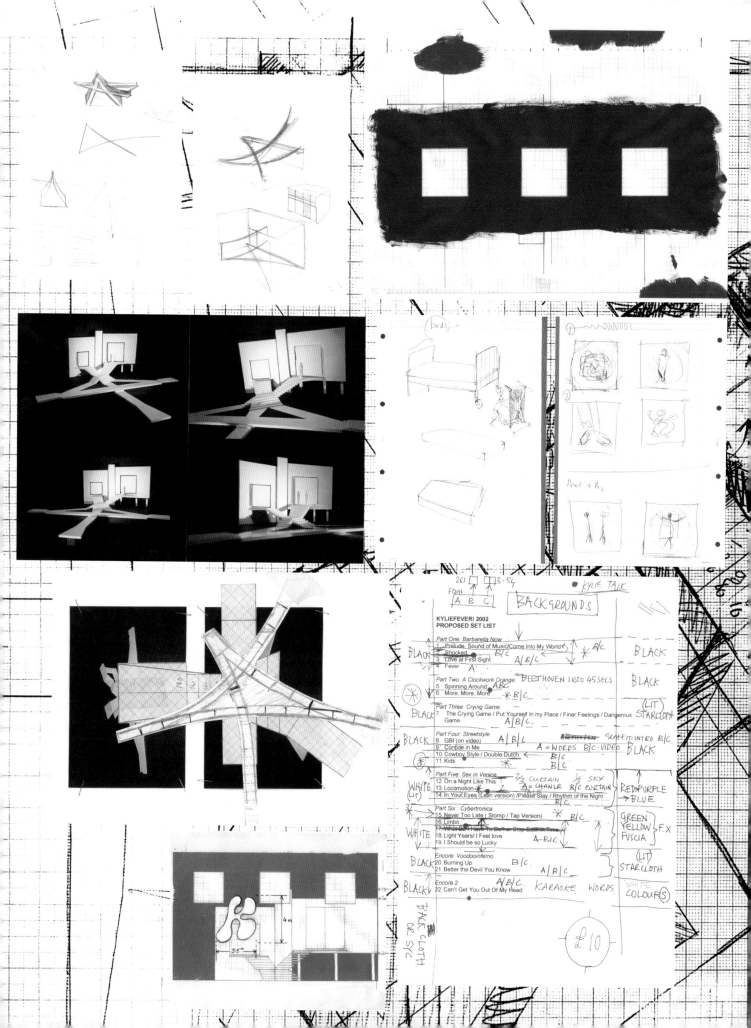

KYLIE TALK

BACKGROUNDS

FROM A B C

**KYLIEFEVER! 2002
PROPOSED SET LIST**

Part One: Barbarella Now
1. Prelude: Sound of Music/Come Into My World — B/C — BLACK
2. Shocked — B/C — BLACK
3. Love at First Sight — A/B/C
4. Fever — A

BLACK

Part Two: A Clockwork Orange — BEETHOVEN INTO 45 SECS — BLACK
5. Spinning Around — ABC
6. More, More, More — B/C

Part Three: Crying Game
7. The Crying Game / Put Yourself In my Place / Finer Feelings / Dangerous Game — A/B/C — (LIT) STARCLOTH

BLACK

Part Four: Streetstyle
8. GBI (on video) — A/B/C — GRAFFITI INTRO B/C — BLACK
9. Confide in Me — A = WORDS   B/C: VIDEO
10. Cowboy Style / Double Dutch — B/C
11. Kids — B/C

BLACK

Part Five: Sex in Venice
12. On a Night Like This — 2/3 CURTAIN   1/3 SKY — RED PURPLE → BLUE
13. Locomotion — A = CHANLR   B/C CURTAIN
14. In Your Eyes (Latin version) /Please Stay / Rhythm of the Night — B/C

WHITE (LIT)

Part Six: Cybertronica
15. Never Too Late (Stomp / Tap Version) — B/C
16. Limbo — GREEN YELLOW FUSCIA — F.X
17. What Do I Have To Do? or Step Back in Time
18. Light Years/ I Feel Love
19. I Should be so Lucky — A-B/C

WHITE

Encore: Voodooinferno
20. Burning Up — B/C — (LIT) STARCLOTH
21. Better the Devil You Know — A/B/C

BLACK

Encore 2
22. Can't Get You Out Of My Head — A/B/C   KARAOKE WORDS — WHITE COLOUR(S)

BLACK

BACK CLOTH OR SYC

£10

As the months progressed, the various Heads of Department came to the table, and they were basically the same crew that had produced the previous year's tour. Steve Martin, production manager, and lighting designer Vince Foster also felt the pressure of the enormity and expense of the task that we were undertaking.

Kylie's wardrobe for the show was exclusively designed by Dolce & Gabbana. Alan and I travelled to Milan virtually every other week for meetings with Domenico and Stefano, who brought their own unique brand of timeless, luxurious chic to the proceedings. They too had little room to manoeuvre within the tightly themed seven-act structure that we had devised. Previously they had designed costumes for Madonna's Girlie Show and for Whitney Houston's tour. We felt like we were in good company. Their attention to detail is paramount. They well understand the symbiosis of pop and fashion, seeing any relationship with an artist as a partnership that benefits both parties.

From the outset both designers agreed that the emphasis should be on fashion as opposed to costume, and they tailored each look for Kylie with their own flair. The first costume for Act One, 'Silvanemesis', had to be minuscule from the start, as it was concealed by the Kyborg Queen's outer shell. Dolce & Gabbana designed a belt-like micro mini encrusted with crystals, with matching bra and choker.

The outfit was accessorised with thigh-length silver boots by Jimmy Choo, that were originally black. Whilst we waited for their factories to produce a silver pair for us, we had to make do by spraying our originals that we had used for the Brits with silver car paint. The boots had to be sprayed three times a week. One night in Manchester, Kylie almost had to go barefoot, as Fran Burns, my latest glamorous sidekick, had resprayed them and had hung them out to dry on the wing mirrors of an extremely large load-out truck. Much to Fran's chagrin (and to all of our amusement), the driver had decided to take the truck on a sightseeing trip around the city, and failed to notice the two boots dangling from his wing mirrors like two huge Bet Lynch earrings. The call was made and the driver, truck and boots returned to the arena with seconds to go.

Fran never had much luck with footwear. In the quick change between 'Silvanemesis' and 'Droogie Nights', she mistakenly dressed Kylie in two left patent boots. As usual the quick change atmosphere was so manic that Kylie didn't notice until she attempted to start dancing. That night she was more hobbling than spinning around.

Kylie's second ensemble was a white stretch jumpsuit with black bowler hat for 'Droogie Nights', a feminised version of the white caddy trousers and shirts from the movie *Clockwork Orange*. Her male 'Droog' counterparts were dressed in white and black boiler suits with red protective boxing jocks worn over the top, and they carried black police truncheons.

The 'Crying Game' dress was beautiful, perfectly capturing the spirit of *film noir* and the ethos of the tragic diva upon which the section was based. The dress was breathtaking, with its plunging laced-up side details clinging to Kylie's every curve, and with its metres of black silk released in a sumptuous fan-like train, with delicate cutaway panels of antique lace. The black silk expressed the sentiment of loss, that love is a stranger to the diva, and that the spotlight can be a lonely place with often only room for one person, a predicament that Kylie knows only too well. I saw 'The Crying Game' as an apt song for Kylie to cover in the show because of its succinct expression of unhappiness and tragedy. The song speaks of loss, loneliness, theatricality and artifice, of all those that have loved and lost, a comment upon the permanent isolation of fame. It is a song that was directly aimed at the gay section of the audience. It had particular resonance for me because of its history of gender blurring, brilliantly captured with typical emotive resonance by Boy George as the theme song to a film that featured a transvestite as a leading lady.

Years before, Kylie had covered Culture Club's ballad 'Victims' at a performance at GAY. As well as a personal tribute, it seemed somehow appropriate for Kylie to sing the words of a gay man, to express the sentiments of love between boy and boy and subsequent loss, and the song retained its sense of sweeping and grandiose pathos.

The song in the show is combined with images of men crying, a deliberate comment on how men aren't 'supposed' to cry. We wanted to create an undercurrent of tragedy, of unhappiness, that succinctly defines the role of the gay icon like Marilyn Monroe or Judy Garland, who operated 'in an emotional register of heightened intensity that seems to bespeak equally of suffering and survival, vulnerability and strength, theatricality and authenticity, passion and irony.' Such women, like Kylie, are described as embodying 'camp', which Philip Core defines as 'the lie that tells the truth'.

The song was particularly relevant to Kylie: the truth of 'The Crying Game' is its depiction of an isolated figure, a thirty-three-year-old woman, who confesses not yet to have reached or experienced pure happiness. The song contributed to the portrayal of Kylie as an anachronistic survivor, a woman born in the wrong era, a lady more suited to the golden age of Hollywood than the modern arena of pop. If anything, the success of the last year has intensified Kylie's sense of isolation. Her journey has been one with more than its fair share of drama, pain and turmoil and loss of a private life: the price of fame. Kylie with her inherent smiley persona conceals a fragile soul and her place in the canon of divas is in my mind totally justified. Paul Watson, who wrote a thesis on the subject of 'queer star worship' with reference to Kylie, says:

for Kylie, 'gay icon' is just another label, a coherent, but hideously generalist way of explaining a melange of different and differently emphasised pleasures, empathies and understandings. With her it is not a career savaging lunge for the pink pound.

Kylie's policewoman ensemble was originally based on the movie posters of Charlotte Rampling's film *The Night Porter*, depicting the actress bare chested wearing nothing but black braces and a military leather cap. The policewoman authority figure came from the narrative of the section in which a New York street kid is seduced into submission by the cop, who is also forced to surrender her ideals and participate with the street gangs. It was *West Side Story* meets *Buffalo Gals*. The police uniform was suitably customised and given the fluorescent treatment and Kylie wore a string vest underneath the pale blue shirt with the 'Slim Lady' moniker on the front, my own personal tribute to blonde Detroit rapper Eminem.

The golden courtesan corset and knickers were pure Dolce & Gabbana decadence, and it was their own boudoir-inspired studio and salon that inspired the décor of the stage for 'Sex In Venice'. Steve had updated 'The Locomotion' following on from *An Audience with Kylie*, which we had all filmed last November. I had a crush on *Brookside*'s Tinhead, so when it had come to selecting audience members to mimic a Locomotion dance, Kylie's eagle eyes picked him out in the audience, and he was hauled onto the stage and made to dance with her in one of those typically excruciating TV moments. Phil Olivier, Tinhead's real life alter ego, decided to gyrate his hips and grinded away behind her. Steve was inspired by this simple but effective choreography to the song, and after my insistence that the 'locomotion' was a sexual position, went on to interpret the song as a sweaty sex fest that owed more to Prince than to Little Eva. It seemed natural in the show for us to push this farther and in true Baker/Macdonald fashion the boy dancers ended up in six-inch heels, black hosiery with a suspender detail and leopard print Dolce & Gabbana Y-fronts.

'Cybertronica' and the encore 'Can't Get You Out Of My Head' featured Dolce & Gabbana's take on the cargo pants, low slung, revealing a G-string. The pants were prominent in the runway show in Milan that Kylie and I attended featuring a collection based very much on Sicilian 'pastoral' chic. Workwear as glamour. The juxtaposition of the masculine and the feminine.

The huge volcano skirt for the first encore, 'Voodooinferno', was again inspired by Grace Jones' collaboration with New York graffiti artist Keith Haring where she cavorted in a ginormous decorated skirt that filled the whole film studio. Likewise, the volcano skirt for KylieFever completely took over Dolce & Gabbana's Milan studio, taking a team of six people to undertake the detailed appliqué and embroidery that gives the skirt its glittering flame-like appearance. The skirt housed twelve dancers underneath, who would be cramped into the airless space whilst Kylie cavorted on the outside, and they were meant to burst out onto the stage at an appropriate moment in the song. On our first night in Melbourne Kylie's skirt, attached to a metal cone-shaped structure by strips of industrial velcro, fell off, revealing all of the squirming dancers beneath.

Make-up artist Caroline Barnes styled Kylie's hair for the show, giving it a contemporary street feel with her decision to style the singer's hair in three French plaits, a style that was appropriate for all the different roles that Kylie plays in the show. Kylie's make-up was similarly striking, Caroline following the philosophy of less is more, and thus giving Kylie a bronzed glow and sheen with minimal war paint. She embellished Kylie's natural beauty, emphasising her lips with a rich deep red and her eyes with shades of gold.

The Kyborg robot itself has a history all of its own. Johnny Rocket and Edward Griffiths designed the beautiful robot, a combination of the *Metropolis* robot, *Star Trek*'s Borg, and Japanese sci-fi erotica. I had commissioned Johnny to make several pieces of jewellery for Kylie, including charm bracelets and the Kylie knuckle-duster featured in the clip 'In Your Eyes'. Johnny and Ed had collaborated with plastics specialist Kees van der Graff, whose own beautifully moulded plastic creations can often be seen on Alexander McQueen's catwalk, and they created the Kyborgs' moulded helmets.

Making the Queen Kyborg's entrance work was another thing altogether. None of us had any experience in robotics/electronics, and trying to get the panels to glide from Kylie's body to create the sexy striptease reveal at the start of the show was difficult. After months of working day and night, we were finally rescued from the clanking oblivion of the scrapheap by bleached blonde specialist Scottie who nursed the sickly Kyborg back to health, swiftly rewiring her just in time for her debut in Cardiff. Consequently the Kyborg became Scottie's baby for the duration of the tour and he was often to be found in quiet moments of downtime polishing her chromed contours with his white cotton gloves.

KylieFever is a celebration of all that preceded it, a pop art fest, glittering, shiny, postmodern in its references and unashamed in its presentation of Kylie as a modern icon. She enters the stage encased in the Kyborg, a robotic cocoon. She is the queen bee at the centre of an electronic hive, her drones gathering and descending all around. She is incandescent, the hard chrome of her outer casing providing a shell, a protection for the soft flesh interface, the delicate female housed within.

Within the two hours of the show she is a Space Princess, a pop messiah, the human element in a world of cyber drones; she is a dominatrix gang leader, the first female 'droog' in the *Clockwork Orange*-inspired 'Spinning Around'; she is the Hollywood diva, alone on stage with only a spotlight as her lover in the aptly titled 'Crying Game'; the policewoman who loosens up and gets down with the kids in a block party; she is a corseted courtesan in a transvestite vice den; an elevated voodoo goddess in the encore; and finally, she is just Kylie, singing 'Can't Get You Out Of My Head'. The whole is a visual expression of the many different ladies that are Kylie.

KylieFever2002 is a joyful expression of self-indulgence. The resulting show is one that is very personal to its creators. On attending production rehearsals Alan and I could scarcely conceal our nerves or excitement at this brave new world that had to outdo the pink palm trees and glitter canons of camp Kylie. Almost one year on since its genesis, we were left feeling exhausted but exhilarated.

Disaster struck when Kylie, exhausted from bouts of extra-curricular promotion that took her out of her valuable rehearsal time, lost her voice in production rehearsals, leaving her distraught and croaky for her opening night in Cardiff. Rescue came in the form of her singing guru Ron Anderson who flew from LA at the last minute with a bottle of potion containing an ancient recipe of Chinese herbs and ume boshi plums which saved the day.

We were all nervous as to how the show would be received, but KylieFever2002 recovered from its croaky start and was sent on its way, thankfully receiving wholly positive praise and reviews.

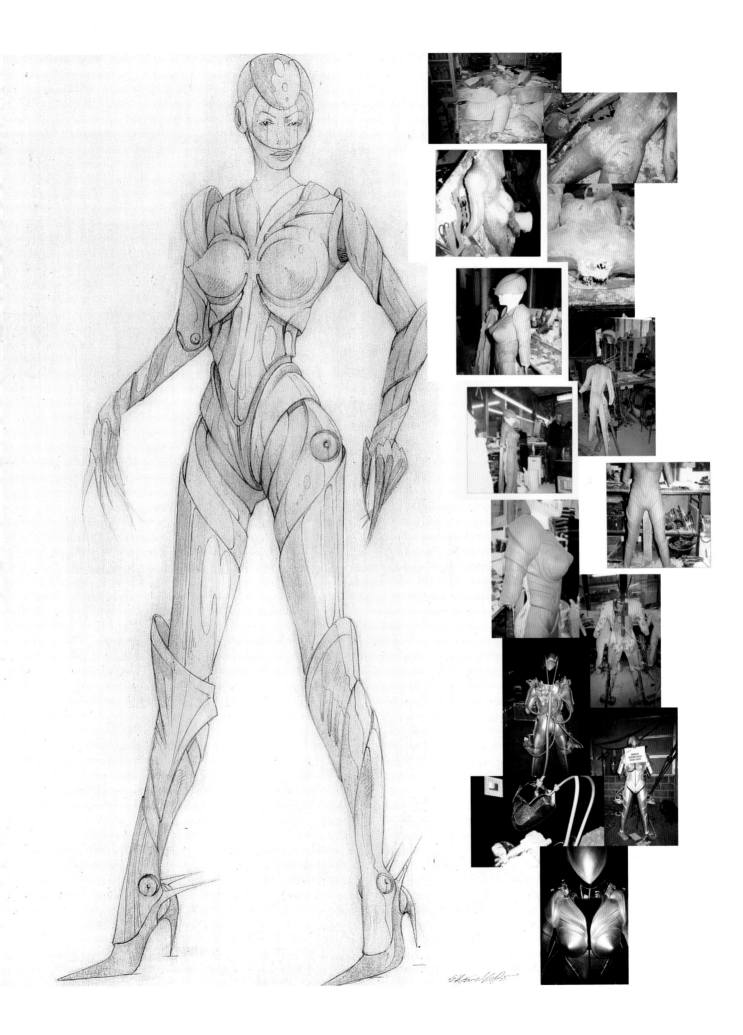

This tour has been the culmination of all
that I have experienced, all that I
have learnt and is the doorway
to many of my hopes for the future.
To work with such a talented and
devoted team is more than I could
ever wish for. Each night, I thank
everyone on stage and everyone behind
the scenes, and they all know that
these are not empty words. I mean it.

When I sing 'these are the dreams of
an impossible princess' at the end of
the show, I realise that they are the
most dreams, and in so many
beautiful, weird and wonderful
ways they have come true.

Both Kylie's and my journeys have culminated in this show. Both of us have come a long way. At the time of writing, the KylieFever tour is enjoying its swansong in Melbourne, Australia, where Kylie was born. It seems appropriate that Kylie's story and journey so far have brought her back home.

Occasionally it is frightening realising we have created a giant, but both of us are aware of the transitory nature of both the pop industry and of fame. I am proud of what we have achieved, of these feats of media engineering that I could scarcely have imagined at the start. I am proud of what we have created: a pop star worthy of our times and of her audience. A pop star whose primary instinct is to perform and entertain.

She has said that I dress vicariously through her and she has enabled me to express many of my fantasies, identities and dreams. I have no desire to perform on stage, but somehow through her I feel that I do. Sometimes it's easier to interpret one's dreams through another person. Facing yourself can be hard. In Kylie I have the perfect canvas for my fantasies.

She and I prefer to work constantly, keep busy, to create and play with infinite possibilities in infinite forms. That is why this isn't a biography, merely a tale - a fairy tale of two Cinderellas. Kylie is not ready to reveal her most intimate secrets and I am reluctant to tell them. We both know the power of mystery and illusion. The person Kylie is can be seen clearly in the results of our work. Interpret in that what you will. Art or entertainment? It is all in the eye of the beholder. Entertaining others or just ourselves, our journeys have been similar, both more accidents of fate than results of the machinations of some masterplan. Fate has been kind, but we have always worked hard and attempted to use whatever resources we had at our fingertips.

My vision of Kylie is really no different now to what it was when we first talked in that coffee shop. We just have more money to do things a little better. Both of us have learned so much along the way. I feel lucky to have had the opportunity to learn and adapt and grow through what became my job. My work with other artists is always tremendously rewarding, but none of it has quite encompassed the passion and sense of mission that I feel when I'm with my diminutive companion. Her belief in me and my talent - something I'd not hitherto dared to trust in - and the freedom she has given me to express myself have enabled me to turn from boy to man. A rite of passage. Likewise, I have watched her turn from girl to woman, from singer into star into superstar. The years have brought us confidence, and the courage to believe in our own convictions. We joke that we'll end up together, sitting with Kat in Shady Pines retirement home, sipping botox by the pool, reminiscing and boring our nurses with our stories about the old times when we were famous.

Our greatest achievement is not work-related - it is our friendship. It remains constant, even though the relentless demands of schedules mean that there is little time these days to chill out together. I think my best times with Kylie are the personal moments we've had together: on holiday with friends in Costa Rica, Miami or Byron Bay; picking up the shreds and tatters of many a relationship gone wrong; drunkenly fighting and arguing over boys in the street. Only then in the quiet times can one reflect on what has happened and feel true friendship's warmth. In times of crisis we have dropped everything for each other. It's comforting to know that if it all went down the toilet tomorrow, we'd still have each other and probably laugh about it all.

The last few months have been like a roller coaster, with little time for reflection, contemplation or even ourselves. True happiness perhaps is elusive, yet satisfaction is no longer a stranger. At the moment the Kylie creation drives both of our lives. Neither of us knows what the future holds. Yet it is that very uncertainty that is so exciting. Each new project brings a new challenge and new experience.

At this moment, as our latest tour winds down, as the Kyborgs hang up their helmets, as the lights are taken down and the sets are dismantled, the costumes are mothballed and the crew is dispersed, both Kylie Ann Minogue and I are content to be led by the star that is called simply 'Kylie'.

Credits

:
Photography: Cover: Robert Erdmann. From left to right: Front endpaper: Xevi, Xevi, Vincent Peters, Katerina Jebb, Katerina Jebb, Ray Burminston, Ellen Von Unwerth, Michel Haddi, Mike Diver, Ellen Von Unwerth, Lorenzo Agius, Ellen Von Unwerth, Marcus Tomlinson, James Martin, Michael Williams, Marcus Morianz, Marcus Tomlinson, Lorenzo Agius, Marcus Tomlinson, Rankin, photographer unknown, Robert Erdmann, Mike Diver, Nick Samartis, James Martin, Lee Jenkins, Lee Jenkins, Marcus Morianz, Michael Williams, Ellen Von Unwerth, Simon Fowler, Robert Erdmann, Adrian Green, Michael Williams, Marcus Morianz, Michel Haddi, Marcus Tomlinson, Vincent Peters, Ellen Von Unwerth, Marcus Morianz, André Rau, Mike Diver, David LaChapelle Preface (005) Jules Kulpinski, i-D 'Beyond Price', 1999 (006-007) Katerina Jebb (008-011) Natalie Stevenson, Natalie Stevenson, Natalie Stevenson, personal archive, personal archive, Brent Wayling, personal archive, Natalie Stevenson, Brent Wayling, personal archive, Brent Wayling, Natalie Stevenson, Natalie Stevenson, Leanne Woolrich, personal archive, Leanne Woolrich, Natalie Stevenson, Natalie Stevenson, Natalie Stevenson, personal archive, Matt Jones Kylie's Intro (012) personal archive, personal archive, personal archive, personal archive, personal archive, personal archive, Noel Jones, personal archive, personal archive, personal archive, Bill Bachman courtesy of Crawford Productions Chapter 01 (016-017) photographer unknown (018) Neighbours, Grundy organisation (020) Neighbours, Grundy organisation (022) unofficial merchandise (025) Sun, Victoria, Daily Mirror, NSW, Daily Mirror, NSW (026) 'The Locomotion' cover, PAL Productions Ltd (027) Sun, Victoria, Sun, Victoria (028) original photography: Simon Fowler, composition: Tony Hung (029) Lawrence Lawry (030) 'I Should Be So Lucky' video shoot, PAL Productions Ltd (031) Lawrence Lawry (033) unofficial merchandise (035) 'Je Ne Sais Pas Pourquoi' video shoot, PAL Productions Ltd Chapter 02 (037-039) Grant Matthews (041) personal archive (042) personal archive (044) Robert Erdmann (045) Tony Notarberandino (046-047) Marcus Tomlinson (048-049) 'Better The Devil You Know' video, director: Paul Goldman, PAL Productions Ltd (050-051) Marcus Morianz (052) Michel Haddi (053) Marcus Morianz Chapter 03 (054-055) Steve Rapport (057) James Martin (058-059) Steve Rapport (060) 'What Do I Have To Do' video, director: David Hogan, PAL Productions Ltd (061) Ellen Von Unwerth (062) Bert Stern, concept design: Baz Luhrmann (064-067) Katerina Jebb (071-072) Ellen Von Unwerth (074-075) 'What Do I Have To Do' video, director: David Hogan, PAL Productions Ltd (076) 'Shocked' video, director: David Hogan, PAL Productions Ltd (078) photographer unknown (079) Steve Rapport (080-083) Ellen Von Unwerth (084) Steve Rapport (086-087) James Martin (088-091) Katerina Jebb Chapter 04 (092-093) illustration: Miles Donovan, original photography: Shoerner, The Face, June 1994 (094) Katerina Jebb (096-097) Juergen Teller (099) Rankin, Time Out, December 1994 (100) 'Confide In Me' video, director: Paul Boyd, courtesy of BMG UK & Ireland Ltd (102-103) Ellen Von Unwerth (104-111) Katerina Jebb (112-113) Ellen Von Unwerth (114) Rankin (115) Katerina Jebb (116-117) Rankin (118-121) Ellen Von Unwerth (122-125) Katerina Jebb (128-129) 'Put Yourself In My Place' video, director: Keir McFarlane, courtesy of BMG UK & Ireland Ltd (130-131) Agent Provocateur commercial, director: Steve Reeves, with thanks to Joseph Corre and Serena Rees (132-133) Katerina Jebb (134-135) Ellen Von Unwerth (136-137) Graham Kuhn (138-139) Katerina Jebb (140) Katerina Jebb (141) Terry Blamey Chapter 05 (142-143) painting 'Ophelia': Sir John Everett Millais © Tate, London 2002 (145-146) David Tonge (147) Kevin Cummins, NME, October 1995 (148) Gerald Jenkins (150-151) David Tonge (152) personal archive (154-155) Katerina Jebb Chapter 06 (156-157) Stephane Sednaoui (160-161) 'GBI (German Bold Italic)' video, Towa Tei featuring Kylie Minogue, director: Stephane Sednaoui, Warner Music (162-169) Stephane Sednaoui (170) William Baker (171) 'Did It Again' video, director: Pedro Romhanyi, courtesy of BMG UK & Ireland Ltd (172-179) Stephane Sednaoui (180-181) Katerina Jebb (182-183) Rankin (184) Harry Borden (185) Mark Mattock, i-D, September 1997 (186-187) Ellen Von Unwerth, H&M Hennes campaign Chapter 07 (188-189) illustration: Richard Gray (190-191) William Baker (192-193) Katerina Jebb (194-199) Simon Emmett (200-201) original stage designs: William Baker & Kylie Minogue (201) Natalie Stevenson (202-203) Natalie Stevenson, Campbell Knott (204-205) Simon Emmett (206-207) Brent Wayling Chapter 08 (208-209) William Baker, Nikos Pap, Sun, UK (212-213) Liz Collins (214-215) Paulo Sutch (218-219) Vincent Peters (220-221) James Gooding (224) James Dimmock, GQ, Condé Nast Publications Ltd (225) Terry Richardson, GQ, Condé Nast Publications Ltd (226) Xevi (227) Rankin Chapter 09 (228-229) logo: Andrew Murabito (230-231) Xevi (232-233) 'Greetings From Camp Kylie' original design: Dick 'n' Si, William Baker, Jasin Boland, Jasin Boland, Jasin Boland, William Baker, William Baker, Paulo Sutch, Paulo Sutch, 'Live In Sydney', Warner Music Vision, 'Live In Sydney', Warner Music Vision (234) original stage design: Jonathan Perry at Perry Scenic Ltd, 'Live In Sydney' Warner Music Vision (235) William Baker (236-237) Xevi (238) 'Live In Sydney', Warner Music Vision (240) original stage design: Jonathan Perry at Perry Scenic Ltd, (241) 'Live In Sydney', Warner Music Vision, Paulo Sutch, Jasin Boland (242-243) William Baker Chapter 10 (244-245) illustration: Richard Gray (246-247) logo: Tony Hung (248-249) Vincent Peters (250) original costume design: Fee Doran aka Mrs Jones (251) 'Can't Get You Out Of My Head' video, director: Dawn Shadforth, © EMI Records Ltd, supplied courtesy of Parlophone Records (252-253) Xevi, composition & illustration: Tony Hung (254-255) William Baker, illustration Johnny Rocket/Ed Griffiths (256) 'Love At First Sight' video, director: Johan Renck, © EMI Records Ltd, supplied courtesy of Parlophone Records (257) Lee Jenkins (259) Mark Abrahams, courtesy of Elle (260-261) David LaChapelle (262) logo: Tony Hung (263) original photography Lee Jenkins, illustration courtesy of Jeremy Joseph for De-lux (264-265) original stage design: Alan Macdonald, lighting designs: Vince Foster (267) original costume designs: Dolce & Gabbana, polaroids: Salvo Nicosia (268) Xevi (271) concept drawing: Johnny Rocket/Ed Griffiths, photography: William Baker, Johnny Rocket (272-277) Stephane Sednaoui (278-279) Nick Knight (280) Lee Jenkins (284) original photography: Leanne Woolrich, composition: Tony Hung (285) personal archive (286) personal archive Back endpaper: From top to bottom: William Baker, Brent Wayling, Kylie Minogue, Katerina Jebb, personal archive, Stephane Sednaoui, William Baker, Katerina Jebb, Katerina Jebb, Kylie Minogue, Brent

Wayling, William Baker, James Gooding, William Baker, William Baker, personal archive, William Baker, William Baker, personal archive, William Baker, Brent Wayling, William Baker, Katerina Jebb, Nicole Patterson, William Baker, William Baker, personal archive, Kylie Minogue, personal archive, William Baker, William Baker, William Baker, personal archive, personal archive, personal archive, Leanne Woolrich, Terry Blamey, Katerina Jebb. Every reasonable effort has been made to contact the photographers, but should there be any errors or omissions, Hodder & Stoughton would be pleased to insert the appropriate acknowledgement in any subsequent printing of this publication.

Text: **Preface** 'Celebrity is about fantasy': Alison Jackson, quoted from an interview in *Observer 'Life'*; 'charismatic authority': Max Weber, *The Protestant Ethic and the Spirit of Capitalism* (Blackwell Publishers, 2001) **Chapter 01** 'I like the bit where she goes...': Chris Lowe, quoted from *Pet Shop Boys, Literally* by Chris Heath (Penguin Books, 1991) **Chapter 02** 'always starring in an endless movie': Marianne Faithfull, quoted from *I'm A Man: Sex, Gods and Rock'n'Roll* by Ruth Padel (Faber and Faber, 2000) **Chapter 03** 'Glamour is defined...': Larry Carr, *Four Fabulous Faces* (Viking Press, 1978); 'fame is a mask...': John Updike, quoted from a feature in the *Observer* (2 December, 1991); 'punk's prototype and...': Gene Krell, *Vivienne Westwood* (Thames and Hudson, 1997); 'genocide peroxide': Boy George, *Cheapness & Beauty* (Virgin, 1995); 'One should either be...': Oscar Wilde, *Phrases and Philosophies for the Use of the Young*; 'sweet kitsch': Kathleen Higgins, quoted from *The Philosophy of the Visual Arts*, edited by Philip Alperson (Oxford University Press, 1992) **Chapter 04** 'I have a massive problem...': Miki Berenyi, quoted from *She Bop II: The Definitive History of Women in Rock, Pop and Soul* by Lucy O'Brien (Continuum, 2002); '"I would rather be...': Julie Burchill, quoted from the On A Night Like This tour brochure; 'In essence, the striptease...': Richard Wortley, *A Pictorial History of the Striptease* (Octopus Books, 1976) **Chapter 05** 'The disguising of the terror of love...': Nick Cave, quoted from *Kylie: Evidence* by Kylie Minogue et al. (Booth-Clibborn, 1999); 'I've always enjoyed...': Nick Cave, quoted from *I'm A Man: Sex, Gods and Rock'n'Roll* (as above); 'the undiscovered country': William Shakespeare, *Hamlet*, III.i **Chapter 07** 'pop star, actress...': William Baker, quoted from *Kylie: Evidence* (as above) **Chapter 09** 'To perceive camp in persons...': Susan Sontag, quoted from *Notes on Camp* (*Partisan Review*, 1964) **Chapter 10** 'With everything changing so fast...': Andy Warhol, *The Philosophy of Andy Warhol: From A to B and Back Again* (Harcourt, 1977); 'in an emotional register...': Paul Watson, *Fever Pitch: Women Stardom and Queer Star Worship*; 'the lie that tells the truth': Philip Core, *Camp* (Plexus Publishing, 1991)

Art direction & design: Tony Hung

Management: Terry Blamey Management

Acknowledgements

:
There are so many people that I need to thank who have made all of this possible and so enjoyable. Firstly, I would like to thank Princess Julia for her enthusiasm, assistance and unique perspective in helping me put this together in an impossibly short space of time. Julia, your insight has been invaluable and I couldn't have done this without you. For that, and for everything else, I am eternally in your debt. I would like to thank the divine and lovely Allison MacGregor and Anna Higgins from TBM who had the unenviable task of sourcing all the photographs, for putting up with my panic attacks and for everything else. Thanks to Leanne Woolrich for sorting them all out in the first place. Thanks to Katy Follain from Hodder & Stoughton for realising that there's no such thing in Kylieworld as a deadline... and for making sure I don't get my ass sued. Thanks to 'boozy' Suzi Dhnaram for co-ordinating the chaos, or at least for trying, and to Georgina Baker and Countess Francesca (Franula) Burns for their assistance, support and advice. Thanks to Terry Blamey for humouring all of our brained schemes and allowing and enabling them to become realities. Terry, your support means so much. I promise to come in under budget one day. Tony 'well' Hung, you have added an extra dimension to everything you have worked on with us. Your sleepless nights are much appreciated. Thanks to Keith Wozencroft, Miles Leonard, Jamie Nelson, Jason Lamont, Faith Holmes, Helena 'u r so darling' McGeough, Murray Chalmers (I never said she couldn't dance) and our extended Parlophone family for believing there is life in the old dog yet. Thanks to Katerina Jebb (damn you, Blake) for believing in me in the first place, for your friendship and the laughs and the fights which still make me laugh, and to Stephane Sednaoui... for forcing me to grow up. Steve Anderson, the campest straight man in the world, Sean 'ten minutes everybody' Fitzpatrick, and all the touring crew of USS *Kylie*, boldly going where no one has gone before, and all the dancers who have had the misfortune of being dressed by me. Andrew Small, Rod Matheson, Chris Pyne and the band. Mum and Shaun Bonner, Dad and Hazel Baker, Nanna and Grandpa, Margaret, Poppy and all my family, Auntie Kath, Linda Tinkler... Thanks to all the photographers and their creative teams we have worked with over the years. Tristan Eves for the camel-ride, Peter Dalton (I haven't changed, honestly). Pete Hadfield, Keith Blackhurst at deConstruction, Mark Farrow and Jon Jeffries. Thank you to all my friends whose constant support I couldn't do without: Alan Macdonald, Kristin Armstrong, Sarah 'monkey' Bailey, Neil Rodgers, Atul 'cha cha' Pathak, 'juicy' Lucy Manning (I miss you: come back, all is forgiven), Paul Flynn (I'm truly sorry I wasn't there when you needed me most), Sarah 'flinty' Reygate, Wayne 'donkey' Shires, Tim Noble, Kurt Jones (I never write, I never call but you will always have a special place in my heart), Travis 'farm boy' Fimmel, Brent 'big back' Wayling, Nikki Love, Leon 'lilo' Lopez, Phil 'if only' Olivier (do the Locomotion with me...), Christian Hutter, Lorcan O'Neill for my education and all the encouragement, Jonathan West, Skiny, Joe Challands (where are you, damn it?), Becky Seager, Ben Arnold, James Polansky, 'sticky' Vicky Bartlett, Jon Draper, Xevi (u r so hot), Matt Jones, Ashley Wallen, Ben Barnett, Natalie Stevenson, Richard 'dikko' Dawson, Steve Shaw, Becca Whybrow and (m)Adam Booth for trying to make a man out of me, Guy 'hardon' Harding, Gareth Davies, Will McNaught and Michelle, Danny Walmsley, Dan Smith, Gail Kniveton and all my old school friends. Thanks to Murray Blewett, Mark Spye, Vivienne Westwood, Joe Corre and Serena Rees, Owen Gaster, Julien Macdonald, Phoebe Philo, Pamela Blundell, Marcus Adams and Baby Cass, Lee Copperwheat, Stevie Stewart, Sandy Gordon, Fiona Doran, Johnny Rocket, Ozzy, Zan Burgess, Patricia McMahon and Polly Strettell (for at least trying to tame a wild beast, and for all the opportunities you presented), Caroline 'barnyard' Barnes, Rafael Bonachela, Luca Tommasini, Shirley Manson for teaching me that there are more colours than just pink. My 'straight husband' Jay Kay (you rock, inspire and brighten up my world, lots of love Monty x), Ester Gill, Cozmo Jenks and 'disco' Dianne Martin, Dawn Shadforth 'beat me on the bottom with a *Womans Weekly*', Karen Alder, Jon Payne, Judy Blame, Philip Treacy and Isabella Blow (for taking a demented teenager under your bird of paradise wings), Manolo Blahnik (what do you mean you don't make shoes in a size eleven?), Salvo Nicosia, Domenico Dolce, Stefano Gabbana, Rita, Giovanni and all at D&G for making me feel like Joan Collins, Robert Forrest, Gianbatista and all at Ungaro, Mark Burnett, Kevin Murphy, Malcolm Edwards and Mary Jane Frost, Boy George (what can I possibly say, but thank you? Love is la di da), Dini, Rossi, Princess Veronica, and all at Bar Italia, George Myers, Ted Bonner (well, you always said I should write), James Gooding for telling us we were crap when we were. Thanks for the inspiration: Marshall Mathers III (from a real Slim Lady to the Slim Shady), Madonna (God save the queen), Bette Midler, Sandra 'look at me, I'm Sandra B.' Bernhard. Carol and Ron, Brendan and Dannii, my extended family — I promise I'll keep my hands off Brin. Alec Mann: I love you. Kylie: I could never even begin to say how much you mean to me, how grateful I am and how I could never be without you. You are the stuff of dreams and legend (and of my nightmares). We are one; we are Borg. If I were a man... I would like to dedicate this book to my grandma, Joan Ellwood, and my auntie, Sue Bland. I miss you, and hope you are both proud. I promise to stop smoking and to not wear any more lipstick.

Love to you all,
William Baker

Ei! Thankyou!

To my family, friends and loved ones. Your
love is immeasurable, your support unbelievable
and words cannot express my love and
gratitude. Please know, because I am sure I
don't tell you enough, how much you mean
to me. Thankyou for everything.

To the thousands of people I've had the pleasure
(or stress!) of working with, thankyou for the
opportunities, the challenges and the trust.

To the millions of people worldwide who have
taken a small or large interest in my work,
you have shone a light upon the space in
which I can create

Love to you all. xx

To be continued...